For 21 years Dr James A. Simpson was minister of Dornoch Cathedral in the Scottish Highlands. During his time there he not only served as captain of the Royal Dornoch Golf Club, but wrote many books, some of which topped Scottish bestseller charts. Dr Simpson is a regular contributor to magazines and newspapers, at home and abroad. He is also much in demand as an after-dinner speaker.

In 1992 he was appointed chaplain to the Queen in Scotland. Two years later he was elected Moderator of the General Assembly of the Church of Scotland.

Dr Simpson has long believed that in any lecture, discussion or debate a little comic relief does no harm, no matter how serious the topic may be.

D1147192

By the same author

There Is a Time to...
Marriage Questions Today
Doubts Are Not Enough
Keywords of Faith
Holy Wit
Laughter Lines
The Master Mind
More Holy Wit
All About Christmas
The Laugh Shall Be First
Life, Love and Laughter
A Funny Way of Being Serious
At Our Age

The Magic of Words

Humorous and Serious

James A. Simpson

Steve Savage
LONDON AND EDINBURGH

Steve Savage Publishers Ltd
The Old Truman Brewery
91 Brick Lane
LONDON
E1 6QL

www.savagepublishers.com

First published in Great Britain by Steve Savage Publishers Ltd 2013

ISBN: 978-1-904246-41-1

Typeset by Steve Savage Publishers Ltd
Printed and bound by SRP Press, Exeter

MIX
Paper from
responsible sources
FSC® C014540

Contents

Acknowledgements

We are grateful to Sir Richard Stillgoe for his kind permission to reproduce his poem "Violin Farm" and to Lucy Berry for her permission to use her poem "Out of a Copper Mine".

To Sally and Jay,
an inspiration to many

Introduction

I have a love affair with words. Whereas some people get tunes in the brain, I get words and phrases in the brain. Words fascinate me. No modern tool or invention is as magical, mysterious or powerful as words. By wagging a piece of red muscle in your jaws, you set sound waves moving. A small receiving set in another person's ear picks up these vibrations, and by an incredible miracle translates them into meaning.

When a friendly postman asked a four-year-old boy, who had come to the door to collect the mail, if his baby sister could talk, the little fellow replied, "No. She has a few teeth but the words haven't come in yet." It is a great day when words do come in, for it is through the medium of words that we can share our thoughts and feelings. Words are the voice of the heart. Dressed up in the garb of an alphabet of 26 letters A, B, C ..., they are the means by which we can access the wisdom of the ages, and learn what is happening at home and abroad. There is almost no aspect of our lives that is not touched by words

I cherish a strange compliment paid to me at the close of a talk I gave. "What I like about you, Dr Simpson, is that you are that simple!" This book is not a scholarly work on semantics. Nor is it an academic study of the development of the English language during the past millennium. The book has been written for ordinary folk like myself, who use ordinary words daily, but are often unaware of their origin, wonder and incredible power. I hope what I have written, and the anecdotes I have used, will interest and sometimes surprise my readers, and perhaps make them think afresh about the magic of written and spoken words. I also hope that the sparkle of humour, to be found throughout the book, will not only exercise the reader's chuckle muscles, but will help illustrate, in an entertaining way, some important truths about life. The comic sense is, I believe, central to what it means to be human. As the poet John Milton said long ago, "Joking decides great things, stronger and better than earnest can." My own favourite kind of humour is that which makes me laugh for five seconds and think for ten.

Parts of this book first appeared in *Life and Work*, a magazine for which I have written a monthly column for many years. I wish to thank the Editor for permission to reproduce excerpts. I want to thank my wife, my number one encourager, for her life-long support, also Kate Simpson for her invaluable help in preparing the manuscript and my friends Bob Sloan and Peter Thomson for proof-reading it. My thanks are also due to my publisher Steve Savage. Working with him has once again been a rare and special pleasure.

Samuel Johnson, who in the 18th century undertook the immense task of defining, in a dictionary, more than 40,000 English words, is quoted as saying, "No one but a blockhead ever wrote except for money." That is too sweeping a statement. The royalties from the sale of this book will not go into my pocket, but will go to support people like my oldest grand-daughter Sally, who suffer from Cystic Fibrosis. My hope is that the royalties from this book, as from my previous books, will help research scientists find a cure for this very debilitating disease.

James A. Simpson

Few Words and Many Words

The Hollywood producer Sam Marx once highlighted how much wisdom can be crammed into four words: "In God we trust; Live and let live; Still waters run deep; Bad news travels fast; Nothing succeeds like success; Nothing ventured, nothing gained; Fortune favours the bold; Man proposes, God disposes; Let sleeping dogs lie." The moral, he said, is: "If you cannot say it in four words, don't say it!"

Once at a dinner, several of the evening speakers had gone far beyond their allotted time. The bewitching hour of midnight was approaching when the person who had been invited to propose the vote of thanks rose to speak. There was an audible groan when he announced that he had prepared two votes of thanks and would like to deliver both.

"The first is short," he said, "the second slightly longer. The first is, 'Thank you.' The second, 'Thank you very much'." What a cheer he got when he then sat down. Unlike the previous speakers he was a man of few words.

Whereas George Washington's second inaugural address as President was short, about 150 words, William Henry Harrison, the ninth President, delivered the longest ever inaugural address, more than eight thousand words. Few recall anything that Edward Everitt, the Senator from Massachusetts, said in his lengthy address at Gettysburg at the end of the Civil War, but what the speaker who followed him said, in 266 words, is an integral part of American history. Abraham Lincoln is believed to have written his address on an envelope while travelling from Washington to Gettysburg. Though he said that day, "The world will little note, nor long remember what we say here...", the world did note, and has not forgotten Lincoln's moving words.

"We here resolve that those dead shall not have died in vain, that this nation under God shall have a new birth of freedom, and that government of the people by the people, for the people, shall not perish from the earth."

The American President Calvin Coolidge was another man of very few words. At a rare press conference one reporter asked him if he had any comment to make on tariffs. "No," Coolidge replied. When a second reporter asked if he had any comment about the farm bill, the reply was the same: "No." When a third reporter asked for a comment about naval appropriation, Coolidge once more said, "No." As the reporters were leaving, 'Silent Cal', as he was known to the media, shouted after them, "Don't quote me." Being renowned for his lengthy silences, when news finally broke in 1933 that Coolidge had died, Dorothy Parker, the American journalist and social activist, is reported to have said, "How can they tell?"

There are on the other hand many people of many words. Eternity has been defined as listening to a six-year-old relate the story of an exciting movie or video. Sometimes you wish little children had come with a zip that you could occasionally pull across their mouth.

That is also true of some adults. By the time they say, "To cut a long story short", it is often too late. It was said of one man that "though he had lost the art of conversation, he had unfortunately not lost the power of speech." Robert Burns knew there were church ministers like that. He spoke of their "three-mile prayers and half-mile graces". Edwin Muir, the Orkney poet, who was brought up in a Calvinistic atmosphere with very lengthy Sunday sermons and services, said, "The word made flesh, is here made word again."

When a man informed his friend that he had not spoken to his wife for a whole week, the friend naturally enquired if they had had a major row. "Oh nothing like that. I just don't like to interrupt!" I can think of members of the female sex who can pack as many words into a minute as a farm auctioneer. One Dornoch woman spoke 140 words to the minute – with gusts of up to 180. The only time she stopped speaking was when her mother started!

Before we fully open our eyes in the morning, or properly gather our wits for the day, switching on the radio exposes us to a torrent of words. Having donned a dressing gown and opened the front door, many are met with countless more words in the form of the morning newspaper. Before breakfast is finished, the phone will probably have rung, and someone miles away, and out of sight, will have spoken yet more words. Later the mail arrives at our home or office, much of it junk. A flood of e-mails exposes us to more and more words. I have often sympathised with the little boy whose version of one of the petitions in the Lord's prayer was, "Deliver us from e-mail." Facebook and Twitter add to the torrent.

Not even Einsteinian mathematics could estimate the number of words spoken, listened to and read each week in Britain. I doubt if the world has ever been so full of words as it is now, all the wordy forms we have to fill in before we can get anything done. I shudder to think the amount of paperwork that would have been involved if the Pyramids had been built today.

Word Play

Though I am hopeless at solving anagrams, the solutions – when my wife points them out to me – often bring a smile to my face, anagrams such as,

The Morse Code – Here come dots;

Britney Spears – Presbyterians;

Episcopal – Pepsi Cola.

Bill Bryson rightly wondered what kind of mind worked out that 'two plus eleven' and 'one plus twelve' not only give the same arithmetical result, but use the same letters, or that 'talcum powder' is an anagram for World Cup Team.

In cryptic crosswords some clues are so obscure that I am surprised that they are ever solved:

'A city in Czechoslovakia' – Oslo (CzechOSLOvakia)

'Orphan, a widely held view' – Panorama (pa-nor-a-ma);

'Side issue' – Eve.

The more humour is a play on words, whether in everyday conversation, or in after-dinner speeches, or on the stage, the more I enjoy it. I hope the following will illustrate the kind of verbal humour that appeals to me.

A professor of English once highlighted the difference between complete and finished. "If you marry the right woman you are complete. If you marry the wrong woman you are finished!"

Benjamin Disraeli defined the difference between misfortune and calamity. "If Gladstone fell into the Thames, that would be a misfortune; if anybody pulled him out, that would be a calamity."

Aware of the danger of expressing negative comments about someone in a testimonial, a director wrote of a former worker who had constantly skived off, "A man like him is hard to find."

Traffic police have been described as 'fine' people, bankers as 'sterling' or 'interest-ing' characters, gamblers as 'bet-ter' than others, steel workers as fine 'tempered', and Inland Revenue Collectors as 'taxing' people.

Many years ago an American lady told how, after she had forgotten to pay her electricity bill, she was sent a reminder. It read, "We would be delighted if you would pay your bill promptly. If not you will be de-lighted."

A woman who reluctantly acquired a new dog named it Greatness. When asked why, she answered, "Because it was thrust upon me."

A Mr. Barner observed to a friend who was an English teacher that when he was with another man he tended to walk through a door first, but when he was with a woman, he always let her go ahead of him. Her reply was a glorious play on the words of an old spelling rule., "I before he, except after she!"

The mushrooming of food and gastronomic meta-phors sheds light on the variety of people we meet daily. Some have taste; others we take with a pinch of salt; still others drive us bananas because they are always in a pickle or a jam. Then there are the hard-boiled, ham-fisted types, the bread winners who make a lot of dough, and others who have to work for peanuts. Most of the attractive people I have known were simple ordinary folk who were not only the salt of the earth, but the apple of my eye. How often in life we truly eat our words!

Lawyers can get debarred. Should politicians be devoted, cowboys deranged, models deposed, and dry cleaners depressed or decreased?

A *Guardian* article on privately-owned coal mines was entitled "Mining Their Own Business".

A story in the *Sunday Telegraph* about the tax man cracking down on company cars was headlined, "The Revenue's 'No Perking Signs'".

Are we the cruellest of all animals? We beat eggs. We whip cream. We strike bargains. We kill with a look. We blind others to the truth, and all the while we are just trying to kill time.

In an article written more than eighty years ago, the writer argued that many animals could play golf, that they are designed by nature for the enjoyment of the game. "The horse often goes out for a long drive. Sometimes however he is inclined to pull, and consequently receives a good many strokes. Hibernating animals have the good fortune to enjoy a good lie all through the winter. The cat can quickly get down to scratch. The lobster is a good pot-hunter ..."

When Churchill was First Lord of the Admiralty in the First World War, he was approached by the head of a women's temperance association. She asked him to reconsider the Royal Navy's practice of christening a ship by breaking a bottle of champagne across its bow. "But, Madam, the hallowed custom of the Royal Navy is in fact a splendid example of temperance. The ship takes its first sip of wine, and then happily proceeds on water ever after."

When a lighting failure delayed proceedings at Clerkenwell Magistrates' Court, a member of the court office staff said, "Justice has to be seen to be done."

July and August are when, in Britain, you finally realise what rainy day you saved for – your holiday.

When a newspaper billboard outside a Highland newsagents bore the heading, "Residents complain – Cows audible two miles away", one villager was heard to say "That must be an all-time low!"

It has been suggested that the surest way to get down to the real nitty-gritty is to eat lunch on the beach!

You know it is time to diet when you nod one chin, and two others second the motion.

Before the days of laptops and mobile phones, it was customary for students at some American universities to leave a self-addressed postcard with the professor, requesting that he mark on it their final grade for the course. The professor discovered that at the top of one card the student had written, "Blessed are the merciful." When the card was returned the professor had written, "Blessed are they that mourn – final Grade: D"

In a Devon village, days of torrential rain caused the river to burst its banks and flood the village streets. Boats became the sole means of transport up and down the main street, called Michael Road. When the waters eventually subsided, a local wag wrote beneath the 'Michael Road' street sign, the words, "the boat ashore."

A woman tells how, at the end of the summer, having put on so much weight that she could not get into her swim suit, she decided to attend a slimmers' class. Having succeeded in losing ten percent of her weight, she was given a prize in a lovely presentation box. This she proudly showed to her husband. The following night on his return from work he presented her with another box. Written on the top of it were the words: "The No-belly Prize."

Discussion in an English literature class focussed one day on how Charles Dickens' life influenced his writing. The professor noted that as a young man Dickens had become a reporter of parliamentary debates in the House of Commons. The professor then asked the class in what way did they think this experience had affected Dickens' later work. One student's wry suggestion was: "It probably helped him become familiar with writing fiction."

The difference between capitalism and communism is that under communism man exploits man, whereas under capitalism it is the other way round.

A businessman was overheard saying to his friend, "My salary now goes into six figures – my wife, son and four daughters."

When a husband on his return home entered wearing muddy shoes, his wife said, "I no longer worship the ground you walk on."

At a medical dinner recently I told the story of two close friends who graduated from an Australian medical school. Despite their specialties being very different they decided to open a practice together in order to share office space and personnel. Dr. Smith being a psychiatrist and Dr. Jones, a proctologist, (a doctor specialising in problems associated with people's posteriors), they put up a large sign: "Dr. Smith and Dr. Jones: Hysterias and Posteriors". The town council was livid and insisted they change it.

So, they altered it to read: "Schizoids and Haemorrhoids". This also being unacceptable to the authorities, they again changed it to "Minds and Behinds". Still no good.

Another attempt resulted in "Nuts and Butts" – unacceptable again."

"Freaks and Cheeks" – was still no good.

Almost at their wit's end, the doctors finally came up with: "Dr. Smith and Dr. Jones – Specialists in Odds and Ends". That was acceptable. It was acceptable also to my medical audience that night.

Humorous Definitions & Adverts

Angioplasty – Inflation you can live with

Archaeologist – One whose career is in ruins

Auto insurance – Wreckcompense

Bargain – Something you have to find a use for once you have bought it

Black skirt – The best thing for removing dog hairs from sofa

Braggart – A person who enters a conversation feat first

Bride – A woman who has ceased to search for the ideal man

Buffet supper – Evening Mêlée

Cement – Stuff that won't set until a dog or small boy runs through it

Censorship – The right to no

Church choir practice – Hymnastics

Clear conscience – Sign of a bad memory

Cosmetics – Crease paint

Cowboy bard – Poet Lariat

Dentist – One who looks down in the mouth

Dermatologist – One who makes rash judgments

Dieting – Trying to be your old sylph

Farmer – A man outstanding in his field

Gardening – Soil sport

Generating plant – Ohm Base

Heckling – Needle craft

History – Gossip that has grown old gracefully

Homesickness – Heartburn

Horoscope – Whither forecast

Housing development – A place where, having cut down all the trees, the developers name the streets after them

Hypochondriac – Singer of popular maladies

Nasty cold – Post-nasal depression

Nursery school – The infantry

October – When the pages of time turn to loose-leaf

Octopus – Cat with eight lives

Perfectionist – Someone who takes great pains and gives them to other people

Pessimist – One who no's too much

Shin bone – A device for finding furniture in a dark room

Soap – Grime buster

Trade secrets – What women do!

Window shopping – Extravaglances

Adverts and notices with a touch of humour

A travel advert: "If you think you can't afford a cruise, you are missing the boat."

A solar energy advert: "The cost of energy rises every day. So does the sun."

An advert in a London market stall: "Square-base cocktail glasses. Guaranteed not to leave rings on tables."

Notice in antique shop: "There is no present like the past."

On the side of a horticultural van: "Our business is growing."

On the side of a bus: "Take twice a day to avoid congestion."

On a market stall in the Glasgow Gorbals: "Feather filled duvets – Buy now before the down goes up."

Sign in a Stirling clothes shop window: "Clothing Down Sale."

Advert for Tailor's shop: "Last of the big time Menders."

Sign in an optician's window. "If you cannot see what you want, you have come to the right place."

A couple tell how when the estate agents hadn't sold their house, they decided to try themselves. They placed advertisements in the local papers. The wife painted a "For Sale" sign which she erected at the gate. When the husband returned from work one night there was a broad smile on his face. "That notice you have painted is the most truthful one I have ever seen." In her haste, she had painted "For Sale by Ower."

The English-speaking nursery school in Brussels advertised itself as "Brussels Sprouts".

Origin of Words

I have long been fascinated by the origin of certain words and phrases – how they got into the vocabulary, and then how by common usage they became the permanent symbol of thought. The word 'sack' for example came from a time when workmen had to provide their own tools. When no longer required by the firm, along with their final pay-packet they were given a sack to carry their tools home. In mediaeval Venice, merchants conducted business on wooden benches in the town square. If a merchant's capital dried up, angry creditors sought justice by breaking his bench, and so putting him out of business. Hence the word bankrupt, from *banca rotta*, Italian for broken bench.

Phrases such as no man's land, entrenched attitudes and firing line all had their origin in the First World War. The Second World War gave birth to such words and phrases as pin-up, holocaust and battle of the bulge. The bombing of Hiroshima introduced further grim words – mushroom cloud, fall out, chain reaction. The Korean War gave us friendly fire, brainwashing, napalm and chopper. Astrology gave us words and phrases like ill-starred and disaster. When the stars were adverse men saw 'disaster' – *dis* being the Latin for against and *astrum* meaning star. Psychology and psychoanalysis gave us words like ego, angst and subconscious. In the latter part of the 20th century, the computer industry has been another rich word factory – software, online, modem. Language is always on the move.

The coming of St Augustine to Canterbury in the 6th century, and the willingness of King Aethelbert to allow him and his monks to win people to the Christian faith had a major influence on the formation of the English language. Centuries later the King James Bible and Shakespeare's plays were two of the major architects in the development of our language. Scarcely a day passes when a phrase from the King James Bible is not on our lips – a labour of love, clear as crystal, the eleventh hour, the root of all evil, a law unto themselves, the fat of the land and countless others. Over 1,900 novels and plays, from Kipling's *The Valley of the Shadow* to such theatrical hits as *The Little Foxes* have titles based on Biblical verses.

What a genius Shakespeare had for words. He made the first recorded use of hundreds of what are now everyday words – accommodation, assassination, obscene, pre-meditated, frugal, dwindle, leapfrog and barefaced, to mention only a few. He was also the source of many common phrases – one fell swoop, play fast and loose, brevity is the soul of wit, salad days, knit your brows, the milk of human kindness, method in his madness, being cruel to be kind, wild goose chase, wearing one's heart on one's sleeve.

Many other everyday phrases and words had their origin in the life of the church. Holiday was a contraction of holy day, goodbye a contraction of 'God be with you'. The phrase 'let the weak go to the wall' had its origin in the days when there were no seats in churches, when the weak and infirm sat on ledges round the walls.

Some priests in the mediaeval church so mumbled the Latin words of consecration at the Mass , '*Hoc Est Corpus*' (this is the body), that these words sounded like 'hocus-pocus'. It is a long way from these sacred words to the formula often used by magicians at children's parties. The comedian's patter has also lost all trace of the original *Pater Noster*, the Latin for 'Our Father'. Saints' days in the old calendars were marked in red. Hence the origin of the phrase 'red-letter day', now used to describe a very special day. The phrase 'giving someone short shrift', came from the Anglo-Saxon word 'shrive', meaning to confess to a priest or minister. A short shrift was originally the brief time of confession condemned prisoners were allowed before execution.

Evolving Language

When in the late 1950s Professor C. H. Dodd and his committee were working on the New English Bible translation, they were stumped in their search for a more modern version of the words 'the fatted calf', the words found in the 17th-century King James translation of the Parable of the Prodigal Son. Finally Professor Dodd went to London's Smithfield meat market with a list of the possible alternative translations suggested by the committee members. Giving the list to one of the market workers, Professor Dodd asked, "Which if any of these terms would you use to describe an animal about to be slaughtered?" The man, having read through the list with care, shook his head and said, "Guv'nor, the technical term we use for these things is 'fatted calves'."

Some words and phrases have a reasonably fixed value, yet because language is a living thing, other words, with the passage of time, often undergo a radical shift in meaning, mainly downwards. You cannot press language forever, like a dead flower, between the pages of a dictionary.

After being shown round the rebuilt St Paul's Cathedral in London, King James II and VII is reported to have said, "This building is awful, artificial and amusing." The architect was thrilled, for these once noble words meant 'full of awe', 'made of art' and 'amazing'.

Plausible originally meant deserving of applause. Now it suggests something specious. Crafty, which originally meant 'adept at one's craft', now means 'not to be trusted'. Though to retaliate was once to return in kind, good or evil, it now refers mainly to evil. Whereas the word 'navvy' now tends to be a term of abuse, it was originally a compliment, a shortened version of the word navigator, the term used to describe those involved in building canals. The word 'prove' originally meant 'test'. The phrase 'the exception proves the rule' really means the exception tests the rule. Far from confirming the rule, it shows there is something wrong with it.

These are just a few of the words that have slowly accumulated the barnacles of negative connotations.

The portly actor Peter Ustinov complained that whereas the word fat used to mean abounding in riches, well furnished, well filled out, with the passing years it had become anything but a complimentary word. Launching a campaign to extol the virtues of being portly, he chose as his campaign slogan,

"A gentleman of considerable weight
Makes by far the best mate."

There are not many words which time has elevated in meaning. Politician, coward and enthusiasm are three of the exceptions. 'Politician' was originally a sinister word. (Some of a cynical disposition might ask, has anything changed?) The word 'coward' once implied a certain degree of bravery. The word 'enthusiasm', which in our day describes a great surge of will-power and energy, previously meant religious extravagance or fanaticism.

An old tombstone bears the inscription, "Vicar of this parish, without ever showing the least sign of enthusiasm." The epitaph describes a steady dependable pastor and preacher who did not panic, the kind still needed by the church.

Careful with Words

For better or worse, words have the power to heal or hurt, to cure loneliness or break hearts. A television programme told the moving story of Mary Grayson, a music teacher in England, who corresponded with a Ray Clarke, a prisoner on death row in a Florida prison. She sat at her desk in England, moved her pen over a piece of paper, then folded it into an envelope and posted it. Ray's final months before being executed were transformed by these letters. He was deeply moved and comforted by the genuine love and concern Mary's words communicated.

Words are the means of showing respect or contempt, understanding or indifference. James, the writer of one of the most down-to-earth letters in the New Testament, reminds us of the power of the tongue for good and evil. "The tongue is a small member, but it can make huge claims. What an immense stack of timber can be set ablaze by the tiniest spark. And the tongue is in effect a fire ... We use it to sing the praises of our Lord and Father, and we use it to invoke curses on others who are made in God's likeness. Out of the same mouth come praises and curses. This should not be so."

Rudeness can cause so much unhappiness and misery. Words that carry a payload of venom have poisoned many a relationship. Temper is one thing that improves the longer you keep it.

The abuse of words by spin doctors is another major concern. George Orwell criticised the politicians of his day for using words "to make lies sound truthful and to give the appearance of solidity to pure wind." One is also reminded of what Humpty Dumpty said in *Alice in Wonderland*, that a word "means just what I choose it to mean." Some spin-doctors, when caught out, bemoan a biased media. Listening to them is like hearing a burglar complain when his own home has been ransacked.

Euphemisms have unfortunately become part of the political spin-doctor's armoury. For centuries, euphemisms have been used to screen the most awful realities. When, in Shakespeare's play, Macbeth informs his wife that Duncan is about to visit their castle, she immediately responds: "He that is coming must be provided for." It sounds so considerate, but what it really means is cold-blooded, premeditated murder, cutting the king's throat while he sleeps. Pleasant words can mask very evil actions.

Jonathan Swift described in the most scathing terms what early colonialism often meant – invasion, plunder, murder and slavery. The Nazis' 'final solution' to the Jewish problem meant committing millions of Jews to the gas ovens. Euphemisms seek to persuade us to endorse verbally what would often sicken us in reality. Friendly fire has become a euphemism for killing our own people. Collateral damage often means that a school or hospital has suffered a direct hit. Economical with the truth sounds so much better than barefaced lies.

'Careful with fire' is good advice, we know
'Careful with words, is ten times doubly so.

Irresponsible words have brought factories and railways to a standstill. Deliberate misrepresentations have damaged countless reputations. Shakespeare expressed it well in *Othello*, "Who steals my purse steals trash ... But he that filches from me my good name, robs me of that which not enriches him and makes me poor indeed." Some American slave-owners suggested the reason Lincoln was keen to abolish the slave trade was that he had what we would now call an African-American mistress. Opponents of the Civil Rights movement misrepresented Martin Luther King as being a communist agitator. Khrushchev dismissed Solzhenitsyn and Sakharov as crazy: "We have no opponents of our system, only a few madmen." The Pharisees dismissed Jesus as a drunkard and blasphemer.

I recently came across a new adjective – 'eristic'. It was used to describe arguments or disputes aimed at victory rather than the truth. I wish more councillors, politicians and churchmen appreciated its meaning. Debates would be less acrimonious. Snide remarks, which demonise and misrepresent those who think differently, would be fewer. Michel Montaigne, the 16th-century French essayist, once overheard two shepherds discussing a controversial issue in the market place of Bordeaux. He was astonished at the clarity of their conversation. Neither of them exaggerated. There was no impugning of motives. They settled their differences and went their separate ways. With that experience in mind, he wrote an essay in which he distinguished between the art of conversation and the art of debate. In it he said, "I embrace the man who challenges me, for he instructs me. Conversation is the mother tongue of well meaning friends. Debate is the public posturing of the self-promoting."

Even when disagreeing with others about Scottish independence, the European Union, and same-sex marriages, we can still be fair-minded and courteous. When in the 2008 American presidential election, a supporter of John McCain called Barack Obama an Arab, McCain corrected her. "No ma'am. He is a decent family man, a citizen that I just happen to have disagreements with on fundamental issues." Though opinions may be mistaken, love and politeness never are.

Gossip runs down far more people than cars. A seat cushion bore the embroidered statement, "If you cannot say something good about somebody, sit right here beside me." Too many enjoy dining out on other people's mistakes and shortcomings. A cocktail party has been defined as an occasion when we eat savouries and nibble away at other people's reputations. Though most people would, if asked, be critical of malicious gossip, yet many seem to enjoy both hearing and sharing it.

Fortunately there are exceptions. A Glasgow doctor told of a fellow flying officer he knew in the R.A.F. He had his shortcomings. He was a heavy drinker and on occasions swore like a trooper, yet he would never allow anyone in his presence to make a disparaging remark about someone not present. As soon as malicious gossip began, he would say, "Knock it off chaps. Leave the poor blighter alone."

Today there is legislation forbidding corporal punishment in schools. But what one cannot legislate against is a teacher lashing a pupil with his or her tongue. Though sticks and stones can break our bones, words can make our blood boil. Sarcasm can shatter a child's self-confidence. It can inflict internal injuries that take far longer to heal than broken bones. On the other hand apt words of commendation can build up a youngster's confidence, and spur adults on to greater effort. If people are to give of their best, they need to be noticed and appreciated. If people's best efforts are met with silence, they tend to become careless and negligent.

Words of love and recognition are vitally important, especially for those at both ends of the age scale. I think of an eighty-year-old whose sons visited very infrequently. They left all the classic signs of wanting to leave shortly after they arrived. Though she knew they led busy and involved lives, yet one day she said to a friend, "It is strange how one mother can take care of four sons, and four sons seem reluctant to visit one mother." What she really wanted to know was that she still mattered to them. It would have made her day had they whispered words such as, "Mum, you are very precious to us."

Compliments can rekindle enthusiasm. "That was kind of you ... What a delightful meal that was ... how well you spoke ..." A professor of English one day got to thinking about a teacher who had instilled in him a love of the English language and poetry. Making inquiries, and finding she was still alive, he penned a letter expressing his sincere thanks. Her reply went as follows, "I cannot tell you how much your note meant to me. I am in my eighties, living alone in a small room, cooking my own meals, lonely and rather like the last leaf of autumn lingering behind. You may be interested to note that I taught school for almost fifty years, and yours is the first note of appreciation I ever received from a pupil. It came on a cold morning and it cheered me as nothing has in years."

For over twenty years one of my prime roles was that of word-maker for the people of Dornoch. I was greatly privileged to be for some their rain-maker during dry periods in their lives, and their rainbow-maker in dark days. Though there were times when all words were inadequate, days when I had to walk into a heartbroken home, or into the Cathedral packed with people with tears in their eyes, I had somehow to find words of comfort that were less inadequate than other words. How emotionally draining it often was.

Speaking and Listening

His thoughts were slow,
His words were few, and never formed to glisten.
But he was a joy to all his friends
You should have heard him listen.

Sometimes at the close of an address a speaker will thank his audience for listening attentively. He is usually being sincere. He is grateful. Everyone has a tale to tell, but not everyone is a good listener. When Simon Callow, the actor and film director, was asked by Chris Evans whether he would have preferred to spend time with Dickens or Shakespeare, he opted for Dickens, because as he said, "Although Shakespeare was a good talker, I believe Dickens was a good listener."

When General Alexander Haig was asked how Henry Kissinger, who had spent most of his life in the States, had such a strong German accent, he replied, with tongue in cheek, "That comes from not listening!" Prime Minister Gladstone was also renowned for over-talking and under-listening. An American journalist seated next to Gladstone at a dinner told how he could not get a word in edgeways. After dinner he was upset to hear Gladstone remark that his dinner companion had been a poor conversationalist! Too often conversation is pseudo-dialogue. We do not listen enough to enable us really to converse.

Attentive listening makes a huge difference in human relations. How important it is for parents to make time to listen to their children as they come in from school or play and relate all the marvellous things that have happened. When greatly pressed for time, parents may have to say "I wonder if you could tell me about it later", but they should make sure first that what they are doing is more important. They should also if possible avoid rushing that sacred half-hour when the children are preparing for bed, for it is often then that their youngsters' thoughts, doubts and questions become vocal. There are few other occasions when parents can get quite so close to their children and share something of themselves, their sense of values and faith.

An Eric Hoffer tells of a Bavarian peasant woman who cared for him after his mother died. He said, "This woman must have really loved me, because those eight years are in my mind as a happy time. I remember a lot of talk and laughter. I must have talked a great deal because Martha used to say again and again, 'You remember you said this and that …' She remembered everything I said. All my life I had the feeling that what I think and say are worth remembering. She gave me that by listening to me."

Being a good listener is a rare attribute. I am sure we have all known times when in conversation with other people we have got the impression that they were not really listening. Their responses were purely automatic. There was no real eye-contact. Their prime concern was to impress you with whom they knew, where they had been and what they had done. Few things are more off-putting, and yet how often we too are guilty of thinking more about what we intend to say, than about what is being said to us, just dying for the other person to stop so that we can tell of our misfortunes or holidays, which of course are so much more interesting.

A Margaret Lane recalls a job interview. The interview seemed to be going well. The director in expansive mood began to tell her about his recent skiing holiday. Eager to make an impression with a tale of her own about skiing, she started mentally rehearsing her story. Suddenly he said, "Well, what do you think of that?" Having heard little of what he had said, she babbled foolishly: "Sounds like a marvellous holiday – great fun!" "Fun?" he asked rather icily, "How could it be fun? I have just told you I spent most of my holiday in hospital with a broken leg." Not surprisingly she did not get the job.

There are five good talkers to one good listener, notwithstanding the fact that no one learns anything when they are talking. On the other hand a listener, someone to whom you can pour out your heart, is invaluable. To listen attentively is one of the greatest services we can perform for another. Thus we can help bear their burdens. Psychologists tell us that it is impossible to distinguish intense listening from genuine love. We may not have what the psychoanalyst calls the 'third ear', but a lot more could be done with the two we have, were we humble enough to listen attentively.

Angry Words

Anger, like any explosive, has both constructive and destructive uses. Many reforms would not have come about had certain courageous people not got angry. As Lincoln watched a woman being sold as a slave, he said with clenched fists, "That's wrong, and if I ever get the chance to hit it, I'll hit it hard." It would be a sad day if moral indignation were to die out.

We do well at times to be angry, but too often we mistake the times. Anger is too noble an emotion to be frittered away in personal animosities. Mistaken anger can be a killer, and not just on our roads. Misdirected anger has harmful physical consequences, raising the blood pressure and pouring sugar into the blood-stream. The major difference between hating and loving is that whereas caring for someone enriches us, hating another diminishes us. Anger also has social consequences. When something happens which threatens our plans, or when we don't get our own way, we are often tempted to bite someone's head off. Such anger causes havoc in offices, homes and congregations. It is the great divider, the poisoner of relationships. Anger is only one letter short of danger!

Does our anger fall into one of the following categories?

Gunpowder anger. The fuse is short, the brows contract, the eyes flash. There is a highly charged explosion. Then almost as swiftly the angry outburst is regretted. Unfortunately, before that happens, considerable damage is often done.

Cold shoulder anger. We punish the one who has upset us by freezing him or her out. Far from resolving problems, cold shoulder treatment makes for the worst kind of misery. Doctors are sometimes tempted to ask patients, not, "What is the matter with you?" but "Who is the matter with you?"

Green stamp anger. For months we collect wrongs and hurts. We keep them alive in our memory to exchange them one day for a big flare-up. The resultant angry interaction moves quickly from the issue that sparked the anger to rehashing past wrongs.

Gang fight anger. When angry we seek to mobilise support. We subject friends, parents and colleagues to every detail of the hurt.

Everyone experiences anger from time to time. George Eliot said "Small things make epochs in married life." How often, when spouses quarrel over something which in retrospect is seen to be trivial, they lose control of their speech and actions. Anger has been described as a brief madness. Unfortunately few know how to express anger without attacking and belittling the other person.

When provoked,

– try to keep your voice from rising above a certain pitch. As the writer of Proverbs said long ago, "A soft answer turns away wrath."

– try to relax your muscles by taking deep breaths.

– try not to talk until your reason has caught up with your emotions.

– try and protect the other person's self-respect and self esteem.

Ask yourself, "What is frustrating or upsetting my adversary. What is going on underneath the surface?"

We may not find an easy answer to this last question, but at least we shall be working towards a better understanding of the one with whom we are angry. I wish I knew who first said, "Speak when you are angry and you will make the best speech you will ever regret."

In conflict resolution the only healthy outcome is two winners. Any time there is a clear winner in an angry conflict there are actually two losers. Shattered relationships can only be healed if the parties are willing to say sorry and forgive. Reluctance to apologise is often a sign of arrogance and immaturity. It is also a sure path to continued estrangement. In challenging us to forgive seventy-times-seven, I believe Jesus was expressing the hope that forgiveness would become a daily discipline, a way of life.

The Inarticulate

Robert Burns' boyhood friend David Sillar tells how, even in his teenage years, Burns had a great facility for chatting up the lassies. He was never at a loss for words. Sillar writes, "Many times when I have been bashfully anxious how to express myself, Robert would enter into conversation with them with the greatest ease and freedom."

Whereas some people have a great facility with words, others have difficulty communicating their thoughts. Some quickly turn to swearing. "He knew not what to say," said Lord Byron of one of his characters, "so he swore." It was said of the boxer Johnny Owen, "He did nothing in his life but box. How sad that he was articulate in such a dangerous language." It was in a discussion about urban deprivation, that I first heard the phrase 'the fury of the inarticulate'. Whereas the majority of people argue with words, some feel unable to do this. Having an impoverished vocabulary, they quickly turn to swearing or to arguing with their fists. I often wonder if we have here the root cause of some of the violence in our society?

Letters written to Social Security offices, car insurance companies, teachers and agony aunts often reveal the difficulty many people have in expressing what they really mean.

In accordance with your instructions you will see that I gave birth to twins in the enclosed envelope.

A driver involved in an accident gave the impression in a letter to his Insurance Company that he had three eyes. "I had one eye on a parked car, another on an approaching lorry and another on the woman driver behind."

Another driver wrote, "I collided with a stationary truck coming the other way. The guy was all over the road. I had to swerve a number of times before I hit him."

In a letter to a Glasgow teacher, a mother wrote, "My son is under the doctor's care and should not take gym. Please execute him."

Mike Tyson, the former world heavyweight boxing champion, was not one of the most attractive or articulate of people. When he was finally defeated by the British boxer Lennox Lewis, Tyson said, "It may be time for me to fade away into Bolivia." I am not sure the Bolivian authorities would have wanted him.

We smile at such 'Foot and Mouth' howlers, but from time to time far more articulate people are also guilty of them.

A notice on a factory notice-board read, "All employees are invited to the Christmas party. All children under the age of ten will receive a gift from Santa. Those who have no children may bring grandchildren."

In a firm's newspaper: "There has been criticism from staff about not receiving company information. To assist in correcting this matter, would staff who do not read this please contact me."

Speaking of Nelson Mandela when he was elected President of South Africa, Dame Jill Knight M.P. said, "Anyone in his position needs to be whiter than white."

Alan Minter, defending the sport of boxing on the radio, said, "Sure there have been injuries and deaths, but none of them serious." A sports writer said of a rugby player, "He played on with a pulled stomach muscle – showing a lot of guts."

An advert in a local newspaper read, "Free to good home – five-year-old cocker spaniel. Loves kids. Daughter is allergic, must get rid of her."

A few years ago an Eddie Russell told in the *Herald* of applying for a job in Queen Margaret University in Edinburgh. On the application form which he received, there was a list of reasons for leaving previous employment. Applicants had to tick the appropriate box. What puzzled him was that one of the reasons listed was, 'died in service'. Eddie said he had difficulty understanding how a deceased person could apply! Then he added, "I can only assume the 'died in service' box was for people applying for dead-end jobs!"

A governor of California, speaking of a dreadful flood said, "This is the worst disaster in California since I was elected."

Vice-President Hubert Humphrey said of the Viet Nam War, "No sane person in the country likes the war in Viet Nam, and neither does President Johnson."

A notice seen in an outdoor restaurant. "Help keep the birds healthy. Don't feed them restaurant food."

When a former Scottish Public Health minister was interviewed on the subject of what steps were being taken to curb binge drinking, she explained that more initiatives were on the way, that soon the Scottish government would be introducing an alcohol bill which, "would include a number of strong measures." She could have worded it better.

An advert inviting people to join a fencing club read, "Join us now. New blood always welcome."

Misprints can be equally amusing.

A notice in a hotel read, "In the event of a fire, inform reception or any ember of the staff."

A boy's end-of-term type-written report read, "English, Fair ... French, Good ... History, Poor ... Mathematics, oGod."

When the manager's P.A. handed him a letter to sign, he inquired how she knew the person he was writing to was small of stature. The reason for this question was that the letter concluded, "Looking forward to hearing from you shorty."

In an application form, a man who had six children and was keen on judo, listed his main hobby as 'marital arts'.

An article about a Mrs. Harrison in an Essex newspaper read: "Mrs. Harrison is friendly, likeable and easy to talk to ... She has a fine fair skin which, she admits ruefully, comes out in a mass of freckles at the first hint of sin."

In the Church of Scotland, the verger or caretaker is often referred to as the beadle. An obituary notice in the *Perthshire Advertiser* commented on the many fine attributes of the deceased gentleman, and the very considerable service he had rendered to church and community. It closed by saying that he had been the 'beagle in his local church.' This prompted a friend to phone and ask whether it was proof that the church was going to the dogs!

In a memo to his secretary, a director wrote of a certain man, "Don't invite him to the meeting. He would monotonize the conversation."

A newspaper interview with a distinguished soldier included a line which was meant to read, "A smile came over the battle-scarred face of the Colonel. But unfortunately it appeared in print as "A smile came over the bottle-scarred face of the Colonel." An apology was printed the following day stating that the line should have read: "A smile came over the battle-scared face of the Colonel."

The magazine of a church in which I was due to conduct the centenary service, informed the members that before entering the ministry I had graduated, not in Maths and Nuclear physics, but in Maths and Unclear physics.

I once had the privilege of playing the very exclusive 'Burning Tree' golf course in Washington D.C. Having had among its members most of the American Presidents, it is known as the course of the Presidents. Each President, beginning with President Taft, had gifted, for display purposes, one of their golf clubs. In the dining room there were also framed cartoons of the Presidents. Eisenhower, Kennedy and Clinton greatly enjoyed golfing at Burning Tree. The club committees were numerous. As well as the usual finance, house, green and handicap committees, there was also a Beautification Committee, with overall responsibility for the appearance of the course. I was amused to see in the Burning Tree brochure that this committee was listed as the Beatification Committee. Was this a glorious misprint or did we have here the genesis of an American Vatican, and Presidential Saints – a St Ike, or even, despite their shortcomings – a St Richard Nixon, St Bill Clinton or a St George W. Bush?

Not only did the Rev. William Archibald Spooner leave us a legacy of verbal somersaults, he gave the dictionary a new entry: the word spoonerism. He was renowned for the kind of verbal slip that turned a 'well-oiled bicycle' into a 'well-boiled icicle'. Though he had poor eyesight and a head too large for his body, he was a distinguished academic. For more than fifty years he lectured in history, philosophy and divinity at Oxford University. His 'tips of the slung' (slips of the tongue) became legendary. Officiating once at a wedding, after the couple had taken their vows, he sought to prompt a very nervous bridegroom, "At this stage it is kisstomary to cuss the bride." At a naval review he commented on the vast array of 'cattle ships and bruisers'. To a delinquent undergraduate, "You will leave Oxford on the next town drain." On visiting a friend's country cottage he is reported to have said, "You have a nosy little cook here." On another occasion he praised British farmers as 'noble tons of soil'. The general consensus is that his verbal slips were genuine, that he was not concealing a dry wit.

Not a Word Spoken

A Gerhilde Moritz tells how once when she was sitting in a Viennese café reading, a young man asked politely if he could sit at her table. Having sat down, he quietly drank his coffee. He then called the waiter to pay his bill. To his astonishment the bill was for her coffee as well as his own. When he explained that they were not together, the waiter apologised. "You did not say a word to each other, so I thought you were married."

A church organist tells how the strangest request she ever received from a bride was for the Beatles' song 'Yesterday' to be played at her wedding. She could not but wonder at the inappropriateness of a song which suggested that yesterday's troubles, which seemed so far away, were now here to stay.

Since the dawn of creation, men and women have not been good at sharing domestic space, be it in the Garden of Eden, or a bungalow in suburbia. For many the phrase marital bliss has sadly taken on the nuances of an oxymoron. A woman in a coffee shop discussing a married couple who were going through a rocky patch, was heard to say. "He married her for her looks, but not the kind he's getting now." For some couples holy matrimony all too quickly becomes unholy acrimony. Marriage once regarded as a sacred bond is now viewed by many as an easily cancelled contract. The knot solemnly tied by a minister or registrar is often quickly untied by a lawyer.

Often little things prove to be the big things in a marriage – remembering to say "I love you", providing an atmosphere in which each can grow, being willing to compromise and forgive ... Little things can also, however, be the cause of big rows. One Glasgow woman told her friend, "We've went and fell out again – ah said the weather's been Arctic and my husband says it's been Antarctic." Another wife tells how one Saturday her husband walked in from the garden leaving some dirt on the wooden kitchen floor. She sighed audibly but held her tongue. "Now what have I done?" he asked. "Did I say anything?" snapped his wife. "No", he said. "But I have heard that kind of sigh before."

The break-up of marriages and partnerships has far-reaching, and unexpected consequences. In an article about reducing our carbon footprints, couples were advised to "Stay together." The article pointed out how separation results in one household becoming two. It means two heating bills instead of one, and consequently more greenhouse gasses.

More than the environment, however, is damaged by unhappy and broken homes. They weaken the other institutions of civil society. They often have a detrimental effect on children. One of the saddest books I ever read was entitled *Torn Lives*. It looked at marriage breakdown from the side of children. Communities can cope with a minority of broken homes, but all kinds of social problems result when the majority of homes become unstable.

Stable marriages and partnerships are not something that just happen. They involve not only finding the right partner, but working hard at being the right partner. Some people's vision of married life is impossibly romantic. Marriage involves much more than passionate embraces. It involves not looking for perfection. When tempted to be intolerant of flaws in our partner, let us remember that we have a few of our own.

A marriage counsellor tells of a woman who talked at length about her marital problems. When the counsellor inquired if there was anything about her husband that she found pleasing or praiseworthy, the woman flared up: "I did not come here to talk about my husband's good points." She failed to realise that one of the basic rules for a happy and growing relationship is not taking your spouse's good qualities for granted.

Other simple rules are:–

If you feel you must criticise, choose the right moment and do so lovingly, not regularly.

Don't bring up mistakes from the past.

Accept graciously the differences in each other

Never yell at your spouse – unless the house is on fire!

Don't let the sun go down on your anger. Avoid colourful sunsets.

Lay off your in-laws

If you have a choice between making yourself or your spouse look good, choose making your spouse feel special.

In one sense everybody marries for 'love'. If what one loves most is money, or position or security, or good looks, or pleasure seeking, then this is very often the love the marriage is based on.

In the casket scene in *The Merchant of Venice*, Portia's father decreed that the male suitor who chose the casket containing Portia's picture would receive her hand in marriage. On the gold casket he inscribed the words, "Who chooseth me shall gain what many men desire." On the silver casket, "Who chooseth me shall get as much as he deserves", and on the lead casket, "Who chooseth me must give and hazard all he has." At first the choice seems like a lottery, the mere toss of a dice or coin, but in fact it was much more than that.

Portia's father was well aware that a girl finds her heaven or hell in the one she marries. Wanting Portia to experience the rich blessing that marriage at its finest is, he was concerned that she would marry the right husband, not a man who had a grab-bag philosophy of life, one who was sure happiness is gained by pursuing purely selfish goals. Portia's father suspected the inscription on the gold casket would appeal to such a man. "Who chooseth me shall gain what many men desire." The outlook of the Prince of Morocco being "I love me and I want you", he not surprisingly chose the gold casket, but Portia's portrait was not there.

Portia's father also knew there are men who cherish a swollen idea of their ability and importance, men who are eager to be rewarded according to merit, for they are certain they merit a great deal. They believe that if everybody just got what they deserved, the world would be a much happier place. It is doubtful if those who think thus have ever done any serious thinking about life at all. What debtors we all are. We drive on roads we did not build. We light and heat our homes with power we did not create. We benefit from medicines we did not discover. We enjoy music we did not compose. What did we do to deserve our physical and mental faculties, all the unearned riches of home, all the nursery songs and stories that opened up into the rich heritage of literature and music? I am occasionally tempted to change one of the immortal phrases in the Lord's Prayer, the phrase, "Forgive us our debts" to "Increase our awareness of our debts."

Portia's father did not want a proud, arrogant husband for his daughter, one who came convinced he was offering Portia more than he would ever get in return. He suspected such a conceited man would choose the silver casket with the inscription, "Who chooseth me shall get as much as he deserves." The Prince of Aragon was such a person. He chose the silver casket, but Portia's portrait was not there.

Portia's father also knew that fortunately there are men who are more concerned about giving than getting, people prepared to go the second mile and do the bit over for those they dearly love.

Love ever gives, forgives, outlives,
Ever stands with open hands
And while it lives, it gives,
For this is love's prerogative
To give and give and give.

Wanting such a loving caring husband for his daughter, Portia's father suspected the third inscription "Who chooseth me must give and hazard all he has", would strike a chord with just such a man. It certainly appealed to Bassanio. The prize was his.

The following are a few witty, but also serious, comments on Marriage.

No man can consider himself truly married unless he understands every word his wife is not saying.

The problem with mixed marriages is not that he is American and she is Chinese, or that he is black and she is white. The problem is that he is a man and she is a woman; that is the mix of it.

Love has the best chance of enduring if lovers love many things together and not merely each other.

A husband and wife went to consult a marriage guidance counsellor. "In our six years of marriage," the husband complained, we have not been able to agree about anything." "It has been seven years," the wife corrected.

Marriage is the world's most expensive way of discovering your faults.

What an outcry there would be if people had to pay the minister or the registrar as much to marry them as they have to pay a lawyer to get a divorce.

When one of the office secretaries became engaged, a female colleague said to her, "The first ten years of marriage are the hardest." When the secretary inquired how long had she been married, her reply was, "Ten years."

Marriage is a place of learning. It is a place where a man loses his bachelor's degree without acquiring a master's.

For centuries in Scotland there were few career openings for Scottish women. Yet it is interesting that the distinguished Spaniard, Pedro de Ayala, who in the late 15th century lived for a period in Scotland, commented on how Scottish ladies were the undisputed rulers in their homes. No matter how powerful their husbands were in public life, in the home the wives wore the trousers. Some men might be tempted to say, "Has anything changed?"

Though marriage is sometimes spoken of as a 'tie', it is actually more a belt, which binds if it is too tight, and falls if it is too loose. Preferably there should be several notches of adjustment to the changing weights and pressures of the relationship.

One thing you learn from marriage is that if an argument begins with "What did you mean by that?" it is not going to end with, "Now I know what you mean by that."

After Franklin Roosevelt was sworn into office a young reporter asked him, "Mr President, are you going to consult the powerful interests that control you in making your cabinet selections?" "Young man," snapped the President, "I would be grateful if you kept my wife's name out of this."

The Power of Words

"By skilful and sustained use of propaganda," said Hitler, "one can make people see even Heaven as Hell or the most wretched life as Paradise." In George Orwell's *1984*, Big Brother, using the technique of the 'Big Lie', succeeds in making people believe that "war is peace, freedom is slavery and ignorance is strength."

Words can on the other hand be a power for good. By exposing in his novels the squalid conditions in the slums, schools, factories and prisons of Victorian England, Charles Dickens brought about many needed reforms. He was a radical crusader against social injustice. So appalled was he on witnessing a public hanging that he wrote a letter to *The Times*. Some believe it was that letter, more than anything else, that brought about the abolition of public executions.

Robert Burns in the 18th century sought to highlight in his poems the narrowness and hypocrisy of those whom he called the 'unco guid', the self-righteous Pharisees in the Scottish Kirk who were enslaved to doctrine and dogma. Burns hated any form of veneer and hypocrisy. He had no time for those who made a great show of their piety. He was totally opposed to the Calvinistic doctrine of double predestination – the idea that it was predestined, before people were born, who were going to heaven and who were not. In his poem 'Holy Willie', based on a church elder called Willie Fisher, Burns speaks of God as sending "ane to heaven and ten to Hell, a' for thy glory." In 'The Holy Fair' he criticises the Rev. Moodie of Riccarton, for mounting the pulpit with 'tidings of damnation'. Burns hoped that through the 'mirthquake' of his satirical verses, a still small reforming voice would be heard. Burns' religious views, deeply thought out and forcefully expressed, helped free the Kirk in Scotland from a deadly pietism and a very rigid Calvinism. The more liberal ministers of his day, including the Rev. Hamilton Paul, who delivered a poetic tribute to the poet's Immortal Memory at the first ever Burns Supper, welcomed Burns' support in their struggle against the extreme pietists.

Josiah Henson was an escaped American slave who fled with his wife and children to Canada in the 1830s. Despite risking recapture, with the consequent loss of life or limb, he returned to the South many times to help other slaves escape. During these visits he met Harriet Beecher Stowe and told her his life story. She was so moved that she put pen to paper. The result was her powerful anti-slavery classic, *Uncle Tom's Cabin*. Though the book was highly commended by Abraham Lincoln, its distribution was fiercely opposed by slave owners in the South.

During the Second World War one of Britain's most powerful weapons was Churchill's ability with words. He mobilised the English language and sent it into battle. He etched on the minds of millions a memorable picture of a defending army giving ground, but never giving up. "We shall fight them on the beaches, in the fields, in the streets ... we shall never surrender. Let us therefore brace ourselves to our duties and so bear ourselves ... that men will say "This was their finest hour." Churchill's words brought new hope in 1940 to a depressed and frightened nation.

Two decades later, Martin Luther King's words caused America to change its thinking about, and its behaviour towards citizens of colour. His words galvanised many into a movement for change.

To speak of 'mere words' is like speaking of 'mere dynamite'.

Simple Words

In the 1940s Maury Maverick coined the word gobbledygook to describe the kind of language he had often heard at Congressional meetings. He recalled one politician speaking at length of "factors in a dynamic democracy which can be channelized into both quantitative and qualitative phases ..." In their desire to sound profound some politicians succeed only in becoming polysyllabic.

Churchill was very critical of those who scorned simple words, substituting phrases like 'lower income group' for 'poor' and 'accommodation units' for 'homes'. One day in the House of Commons, on hearing an M.P. use the phrase 'accommodation unit', he startled M.P.s by exploding into song: "Accommodation Unit, Accommodation Unit, there's no place like Accommodation Unit."

"Short words are best," Churchill said, "and the old words are best of all."

Benjamin Franklin told how when he was a boy, he said to his mother one day, "I have imbibed an acephalous molluscus." His mother got such a shock, not realising he was simply saying, "I have eaten an oyster", that Franklin there and then resolved never again to use big words when little words would do.

During the early years of the Second World War the American General Services Administration placed a poster in every room in Federal office buildings. When a proud bureaucrat read the wording of the poster to President Roosevelt, "It is obligatory that all illumination be extinguished when the premises are vacated", Roosevelt's reaction was, "Why cannot they simply say, 'Put out the lights when you leave?'" Thirty years later President Carter issued an instruction that Federal regulations be written in simple English. In light of this instruction, one planning division in California hired a specialist in plain writing. His blue pencil simplified many words. He substituted the word use for utilise, start for inaugurated, and now for 'at this point in time'.

I was reminded of this when I read the small print of an insurance company's Life Policy. "Each contractual premium contains a provision against possible adverse changes in mortality experience." Did they not simply mean 'death'?

One of Britain's largest translation companies tells of receiving a phone call enquiring whether they translated English. When they asked into what language, they were surprised when the client said, "Into English." Unable to make sense of the lease purchase agreement on her new car, she had decided to call in professional help.

Simon Winchester's fascinating story *The Professor and the Madman* is based on the most ambitious linguistic project ever undertaken – the publication of the twenty-volume *Oxford English Dictionary*. For many years the editor, Professor James Murray, the son of a

Hawick tailor, was unaware that Dr. William Minor, one of his most valued researchers, was a long-term inmate of Broadmoor mental hospital. During the American Civil War, in which Dr. Minor had served as a medical officer, the sight of countless mutilated bodies, and seeing the letter D being branded on the faces of deserters with a hot poker, unhinged his mind. For the rest of his life he was plagued with violent flashbacks. Convinced people were trying to harm him, he came to London. There one night he shot and killed George Merrett, a father of six, a man he mistakenly thought was trying to break into his house.

Dr. Minor spent the rest of his life in Broadmoor Mental Hospital. Early in the project Dr. Murray sent instructions to Dr. Minor and others who had volunteered to help with the massive research programme: "There must be no words in the definition more complicated or less likely to be known than the word being defined." In other words, definitions were to be as simple as possible.

Are not most of us guilty at times of using elaborate phrases when simpler words would suffice? How often in the minutes of committee meetings, instead of the word 'thank', the phrase 'express deep gratitude' is used. Instead of 'end' we use 'draw to a close'; instead of 'discuss' we talk of 'giving consideration to the question of'; instead of 'before', we write 'prior to the commencement of'.

C. S. Lewis said, "Any fool can write learned language. The vernacular is the real test". He once suggested that a condition for becoming a preacher should be the passing of an examination in translation from scholarly language into the language of ordinary people. I would say Amen to that. I remember it being said of one church minister that his members were tempted to take three books to church – their Bible, Hymn book and dictionary!

Robert Burns had the ability of expressing the profoundest of thoughts and the deepest of feelings in gloriously simple language. His love poems are among the finest in the world.

As fair art thou, my bonnie lass,
So deep in luve am I;
And I will luve thee still, my Dear
Till a' the seas gang dry.

Till a' the seas gang dry, my Dear
And the rocks melt wi' the sun;
O I will love thee still my Dear,
While the sands o' life shall run.

What magnificent simplicity. Only seven of the words in the whole poem are not monosyllables.

I love the story of the artist who was painting a farm scene. The farmer watched him with great interest. At one stage the artist said to the farmer, "You have lived close to nature all your life, so you probably have seen her ever-changing pageant, the lambent flames of dawn, the sulphurous cloud-isles in a sea of fire at sunset, and her raven-black storm demons prowling the sky." "No," replied the farmer, "not since I gave up drinking."

Hearing an American reporter stressing the need for clarity and simplicity in language, so that what is said should not be misunderstood, a Londoner said, "What about your use of the word 'fix'? When invited to dinner in the States the host will likely ask how you would like your drink fixed. Does he not mean mixed? When the hostess calls you to hurry because dinner is all fixed, does she not mean prepared or ready? When another guest at the table says he must get his flat tyre fixed, does he not mean repaired? When Americans say they are on a fixed income do they not mean a steady or unchanging income? And when you say, 'I'll fix him' – do you not mean you will somehow get revenge. It is sometimes not easy to follow their simplifications!"

It is no different with what was originally an American word – 'O.K.' It can serve as an adjective, (the meal was O.K.), or as a verb, (can you O.K. this?), or as a noun, (I need your O.K.), or as an adverb, (We played O.K.). But let us not be too hard on the Americans. We also have nouns that become verbs, and verbs nouns. We too have versatility in the meaning of words. The word 'fly' signifies not only an annoying insect, but a method of travelling or a part of a man's trousers. 'Dribbling' is a term for weaving a soccer ball past defenders, but also for an involuntary excess of saliva flowing from the mouth. The word 'keep' often means retain, but it can also mean continue – "keep cool or keep smiling".

I warm to the child's question, "Why do grown-ups use such big words to say such easy things?" The child in me also wants to ask:

– why is 'abbreviation' such a long word?

– why isn't 'phonetic' spelt the way it sounds?

– should there not be a shorter word for 'mono-syllabic'?

– whose cruel idea was it for the word 'lisp' to have an 's' in it?

– why does four have a 'u', but not forty?

English can be a puzzling language. It has so many words which although spelt the same way, yet sound very different. Early – dearly; four – tour; paid – said. The following sentences and a verse of doggerel highlight how maddeningly inconsistent English is:

The bandage was bound round the wound. The insurance was invalid for the invalid. The wind was too strong to wind the sail.

Beware of heard, a dreadful word,
That looks like beard, and sounds like bird.
And dead; it's said like bed, not bead,
For goodness sake, don't call it deed.

The Joy of Reading

In his biography of Abraham Lincoln, Carl Sandburg tells how, though Lincoln had very little formal education, during his teenage years he read everything he could lay his hands on. He read the Bible, the only book his parents possessed. He borrowed and read *Aesop's Fables*, *The Pilgrim's Progress* and the *Life of George Washington*. On one occasion he walked twenty miles to borrow a book from a lawyer. Books, said Sandburg, greatly enriched Lincoln's life. The humorous writings of Josh Billings brightened his dark hours. Lincoln said of Billings, "Next to William Shakespeare he is the greatest judge of human nature the world has ever seen."

When Benjamin Franklin was once asked, "What kind of person deserves to be most pitied?" he replied, "A lonely person who on a rainy day does not know how to read."

My wife, for whom reading is a favourite activity, would agree. "You are never lonely," she told our children, "if you have a good book." Helen loves when friends share a book they have greatly enjoyed, or introduce her to a new author. When we visit a book-shop or library, though I head for the biography section, and Helen for the fiction section, we share a common love of books written by authors who sound like friends talking to us, sharing their experiences about the depth, preciousness and mystery of life. We both feel about bookshops and libraries what some people feel about jewellers or clothes shops. It saddens us when we hear of one closing.

Lin Yutang, a favourite author of mine, wrote, "There are two kinds of reading, reading out of business necessity, and reading as a luxury. The second kind partakes of the nature of a secret delight. It is like a walk in the woods, instead of a trip to the market. One brings home not packages of canned tomatoes, but a brightened face and lungs filled with good clean air."

Dealing with memos flooding your desk is one thing. Sitting down quietly at home and slowly reading yourself into another world, is quite different. Many have dated the start of a new chapter in their life from the reading of a book. Books make it possible on a damp cold January day to travel to sunnier climes. They help us learn who we are, and to what we might aspire. Books transport us back in time and introduce us to people like Gandhi, Lord Shaftesbury, Father Damien, Jesse Owens and Anne Frank. They make it possible to visit Auschwitz and in our minds witness not only the smoke rising from the chimneys, but the fearful depths to which human beings can sink. Dickens' *Tale of Two Cities* makes it possible for us to climb the steps of the guillotine with Sydney Carton, as he went to that 'far, far better rest than he had ever known'.

Aristotle greatly enriched life for many by making Alexander the Great a reader and champion of books, for this ultimately led to Alexander's successor Ptolemy I building the world's first great library in Alexandria. Centuries later Colonel James Anderson, by opening his private library to working boys in Pittsburgh, unwittingly had a profound effect on the lives of millions of readers, for one of the most regular visitors to his library was the young Andrew Carnegie. Carnegie, who was a cotton boy at the time, came to recognise at an early age the benefit of free libraries. What a major impact this had on his philanthropic work years later. Before his death Carnegie had gifted over three thousand public libraries. His boast was justified that the sun never set on one of his free libraries. Edinburgh, Pittsburgh, Dunfermline, Dallas, Dunedin, Dornoch were just a few of the many towns and cities which benefited from the gift of a library. Above the entrance to all of them are carved the words "Let there be light."

Word Sounds

Some words don't sound right. Pineapple is such a word. If ever there was an object that looked less like pine nuts and less like an apple, pineapple must be it. Grapefruit is another such word. If someone handed me an unfamiliar fruit that was yellow, sour and the size of a cannonball, I don't think I would say, "Well it is rather like a grape."

Other words, however sound just right for the things they describe – chortle, dribble, drudgery, slush, galoshes, globule, bleak, grim, to mention just a few. Churchill coined the name of Quisling, the Norwegian collaborator with the Nazis, as a synonym for traitor. In one of his famous speeches he spat out the words, "These vile quislings in our midst." He was certain the word sounded right for the kind of turncoats to whom he was referring.

Grudge is another such word, both noun and verb. Its very sound echoes its unattractive meaning. To bear a grudge, to retreat into bitterness is to live in self-inflicted torture. Some unhappy people have too good a memory for the wrong things, for every slight, real or imaginary. They keep stirring their unhappy memories like a witch's potion, regularly adding new grievances. Such constant retelling helps grudges fester. Grudges can in turn cloud our judgement.

Memories of hurtful things said or done to us, can impoverish our lives. They can, as the poet Coleridge said, work 'like madness in the brain'.

Getting revenge never evens the score. It simply ties all concerned into an endless spiral of retaliation. Though the willingness to forgive may not always succeed in overcoming enmity, it at least breaks the vicious chain reaction. For our own state of health it is important we get the grudge virus out of our system.

In the strip cartoon, Andy's stage boss kept slapping him across the chest when they met. Finally Andy had had enough. He said to his friend Amos, "I am going to put a stick of dynamite in my shirt-pocket, so that the next time he slaps me, he is going to get his hand blown off." He seemed not to realise that in the process he would destroy himself.

To those who bear a grudge, who are convinced they have a genuine grievance, I would say, "Don't put it in a glass case and gloat over it. You will travel with a lighter heart and surer foot without it."

We are told Abraham Lincoln never remembered a wrong done to him, and never forgot a kindness. What a consecrated use of memory.

Kindly Humour

Writing in the 1930s about the European dictators, the Chinese philosopher Lin Yutang told of a journalist who interviewed Mussolini. When the draft typescript was submitted to be passed for publication, the words "Mussolini laughed" were crossed out, prompting Yutang to ask, "Must they look frightfully serious in order to keep themselves in the saddle?" Lin Yutang knew that power without humour is almost as dangerous as power without honour.

Many authoritarian figures cannot tolerate a jest that has them as its object. Charles de Gaulle once threatened with imprisonment a Parisian cartoonist who regularly portrayed him as a clown. Whereas some British politicians welcomed the publicity resulting from appearing on 'Spitting Image', others were upset when the 'upstart' producer or script writer highlighted their idiosyncracies.

A former American vice-president Bob Dole had a highly developed sense of humour. When some of his light-hearted and humorous comments appeared in print, he would receive critical letters inferring that his remarks indicated a lack of seriousness! Far from being suspicious of such politicians, I warm to those who use humour to highlight the incongruities and occasional absurdities of political life.

When Martin Buber, the brilliant Jewish thinker, was asked why the Christian world took his writings more seriously than the Jewish world, he replied with a twinkle in his eye, "Jews are smarter." Such self-deprecating humour is a mark of maturity, a sign of sanity and a preserver of it. Self-deprecating humour is the healthiest brand of humour, the only target being yourself.

I wish humour had been included with the other five senses, for a sense of humour helps us see things, and ourselves, more in perspective. Too many aspiring politicians and aloof scholars view themselves with disproportionate immodesty. As long as we can laugh at ourselves there is hope for us and the things we hold dear. It is when we lose that capacity that we begin to lose our footing.

Whereas there is nothing funny about cruel humour, derision and sarcasm always being at someone's expense, more kindly humour can be a powerful instrument in the service of truth and needed reforms. I agree with Churchill – "You cannot understand the most serious things in life unless you understand the most humorous."

Kindly laughter is one of the best solvents for the grit of irritation which regularly gets into the cogs of life. People without a sense of humour tend to be like wagons without springs, jolted and upset by every bump on the road of life.

Humour can help remind us that "we see in a mirror dimly", that "we know in part" and "prophesy in part." The alternative to humour is the arrogance and idolatry of those who profess to see clearly, know absolutely and prophesy infallibly. Faith without humour, like power without humour, can quickly become a prey to intolerance. It can spawn hatred and conflict. Some of the most dangerous people in our world today are fanatical humourless Christians, Jews and Muslims who are certain they alone are right. They fight evil as if it were something totally outside themselves. A sense of humour can protect us from delusions concerning our own righteousness and superior virtues. Religion can be deadly if it has no humour.

When a friend of Voltaire's overheard him speaking highly of a contemporary, he said, "It is good of you to say such pleasant things about him when he says such unpleasant things about you." Whereupon Voltaire suggested, "Perhaps we are both mistaken!" Though a sense of humour doesn't remove obstacles from our paths, or solve all our problems, or protect us from criticism, it does help us cope better. I could not have survived in the ministry for more than forty years, had I not had the ability to laugh at my own pretensions and foibles, and to laugh more quietly at the foibles and pretensions of some of my members.

What a saving grace kindly humour is.

Misunderstandings

Though misunderstandings can sometimes have painful consequences, they can also occasionally be the source of much laughter. I think of the prim little lady who enquired at a travel agency about a possible summer tour. When the agent mentioned that this particular tour included the Passion Play at Oberammergau, the woman drew herself up to her full five-feet-one and replied icily, "I am sick and tired of all this sex stuff" – and stormed out.

Having decided that the order he had made for sixty turkeys for the staff Christmas dinner was more than would be needed, the manager of the large office canteen, telephoned the suppliers and asked them to cut the order in half. Two days before Christmas the order was received. Sure enough: sixty turkeys, all neatly cut in half.

A minister who felt that his morning service had gone well, and had not been too long, was surprised when a lady visitor said, or appeared to say, as she shook hands with him at the door, "I'm glad it's done." Later he was greatly relieved when he realised that what she had said was, "I'm Gladys Dunn."

At her birthday party, an eighty-year-old great-grandmother, having told her family and friends that she had received flowers from Interpol, added, "I don't know how they got my address." On hearing this one of her grandsons said, "Interpol would certainly have a record of your address, for you are one of the most wanted grandmothers in the world."

On a flight to an international congress at which a professor was to give a talk on physical fitness, he sat next to an Australian in his mid-thirties. During their conversation, the Australian suddenly announced that he was fifty pounds overweight. The professor, eyeing the man's rather plump figure, said, "Oh, I would not say fifty, but you could certainly lose twenty." To the professor's embarrassment the man snorted, "I'm talking about my luggage, not my body!"

A six-year-old boy, who was visiting the library with his mother, asked the librarian for her help in finding a puppy training video for his new beagle puppy. When he returned the video, she asked him if it had helped. "Not really," he said. "I could not get my puppy to watch it for long. At his age, he's mostly interested in food, you know."

In 1934 the local Southport newspaper, *The Southport Visitor*, highlighted a misunderstanding which arose in the Southport school which overlooked Royal Birkdale Golf Club. From her classroom window seat, Marion who was a keen golfer, suddenly caught a glimpse of Henry Cotton, the finest British golfer of his day, playing golf with the Prince of Wales. At the very moment she was observing them, the teacher asked the class, "Where do you find cotton?" "On the golf course with the Prince of Wales," answered Marion." Though the teacher was not amused, the local newspaper editor on hearing the story thought it was well worth sharing.

A Jim Thomson recalls a mother who had to tell her eight-year-old son that their labrador dog Laddie had died during the night. Instead of the expected flood of tears and broken heart, there was a quiet acceptance. Off to school he went with a kiss and a hug. On his return the first thing he asked was "Where's Laddie?" Mum told him again that Laddie had died. Now tears and awful sobs ensued. Eventually she asked why he had not been upset in the morning. He replied, "I thought you said Daddy had died."

When a Russian translator was confronted with the Biblical phrase "The Spirit is willing, but the flesh is weak", he hesitated for a moment before translating it, "The vodka is all right but the meat is underdone."

When Steinbeck's book *The Grapes of Wrath* was published in Chinese, it first appeared under the title *Angry Raisins*.

The former Minister of Defence, Sir Malcolm Rifkind recalls a mistranslation into Swedish of the proverb 'Out of sight, out of mind'. It came out as 'Invisible and Crazy'.

The idea for the name of the central character of Dickens' *Christmas Carol* came about as a result of a misunderstanding. During a visit to Dundee, Dickens observed in a cemetery a headstone on which were inscribed the words "Ebeneezer Scroggie, a Meal man."

Perhaps because of moss on the stone or poor eyesight, he read it as a Mean man. The name Scroggie he changed to Scrooge.

A mother tells how when her son Gregory was eight years of age, he could conceive of no greater pleasure than to be allowed to mow a lawn. During a seaside holiday he found a push mower in the shed of their rented cottage. He mowed the cottage lawn every second day. While mowing, he would cast covetous eyes at the long grass next door. One day Gregory's mum saw him talking over the fence to the man in the neighbouring cottage. Coming into the house looking crestfallen, she asked him what was wrong. "Well," said Greg, "he wanted to know if I would like to mow his lawn and I said, 'Yes'. Then he said to me, how much? But I had not any money!"

A Brownie Guide who had attended a special St. George's Day church service told her mother how at the end of the service they had all stood and sung the Grand National.

The broad Glasgow accent can sometimes be misunderstood, with disastrous consequences. When a Scottish stewardess on a plane bringing holiday makers from Malaysia to Gatwick asked a question of an English couple, the woman retorted irately, "How dare you ask me if we've had sex." The stewardess tried to explain: "I was asking, 'Have you headsets', the kind for listening to in-flight entertainment."

When a Glasgow woman asked the immigrant Polish bus driver in Edinburgh for a 'Noddy ticket', he stared blankly at her. She then sought to explain, "A friend told me to ask for a noddy ticket." Still there was a blank look on the driver's face. At that a West of Scotland man sitting behind her spoke up. "She wants an a'day ticket."

One scorching hot summer day an 81-year-old woman, who was proud of the fact that she did not look her age, went to the chemist's. Referring to the very warm weather, she said to the assistant, "Going to be eighty-seven today." She was mortified when the chemist reached across the counter, shook her hand and said, "Happy Birthday."

A blind man with a guide dog was standing outside a shop one day with a collecting can. A little lad went over and dropped a coin into his can. When his mother took his hand to lead him away, he burst into tears, and would not stop crying. Finally the mother shouted back to the collector that her son had been under the impression he had bought the dog.

Once Upon a Time

Abraham Lincoln, who was renowned for telling stories, said, "They say I tell a great many stories. I reckon I do, for I have learned from experience that people are more easily influenced through the medium of a story than in any other way." Lincoln knew that stories linger in the memory far longer than abstract statements. Truth becomes intimate and evocative when presented in the guise that we humans know best – the story. The New Testament not only records many of the stories Jesus used, it tells us that he never spoke to the crowds without a story. He knew stories can help us make sense of our lives. They can also help us remember what we might otherwise quickly forget

A teacher tells how a team of painters working on the outside of their nursery school managed each morning to be working near an open window when the radio programme 'Story Time' began. Brushes were put down. They rested their elbows on the window sills and listened with rapt attention. One morning before school started, a young painter approached the teacher. Looking somewhat abashed, he said, "I was off sick yesterday, so I missed out on the story. Tell me, what did happen to the little red dragon?"

I learned, at an early age, the delight of listening to an outstanding story-teller. My mother, who for many years was the headmistress of a school in Hamilton for children with disabilities, was such a person. She and my father did not marry until they were almost forty. She would tell us bed-time stories about her childhood, about what it was like when she was young, her favourite toys, the games she played. We also loved hearing about the deaf, dumb and blind children she had helped and taught, especially stories about the tumbling clowns they made, and about one little boy who travelled at breakneck speed, despite having had both legs amputated. Strapped to his bottom was a very early kind of skateboard. These stories had a special magic for me. I could well imagine my mother saying to today's mothers, "Forget the news on television; it will always be there with its load of depressing information. Forget the ironing which by its very nature is never done. Make time to sit down in an armchair with your children, or by their bedside, and tell them a story." She would have agreed with the poet John Masefield who spoke of stories being as necessary for children as fresh air. There are few more entrancing words than "Once Upon a Time."

Recently a story written by a Mrs. Hersey interested me. She told of visiting friends whose little girl put on an 'I'm sick' act every morning at breakfast in an attempt to stay at home from school. Her parents fretted that she had serious health problems, even though the doctor had reassured them that there was nothing wrong with her. "When it was my turn to put her to bed," wrote Mrs. Hersey, "I tried a variation of the Aesop fable, the boy who cried wolf. I told her about Anne, a little girl who did not like school and would pretend to be sick in the mornings. My little audience watched me cautiously from her pillow, but was quickly caught up in the narrative. Anne developed a tummy-ache at school, but the teacher wouldn't believe her because she was always saying she was ill, when she was not. Eventually only when Anne collapsed in the classroom did anyone believe her. I finished with 'And Anne never again said she was feeling ill when it was not really true.' My little listener then settled down to sleep. In the morning at breakfast she looked thoughtfully across the table at me and began eating her cereal. For the first time in weeks, she went off to school without complaint."

My father regularly read stories to us in the old unlicensed Fiat that sat in our driveway. There Dad introduced us to the wonderful short stories of Leo Tolstoy, and the American writer O'Henry. Many of these short stories made a deep impression on me, none more so than O'Henry's story about a thief who sat one evening smoking a cigar in a park. That day he had swindled a child out of a dollar bill for breakfast, and tricked an old man out of a wad of notes for dinner. He sat chuckling at the thought of his successful day. Just then a young woman passed hurrying home. She was dressed in white. There was a purity and honesty about her face. Several years previously he had sat on the same bench with her at school. What a lovely girl she had been. What happy times they had had together. Suddenly he got up, laid his burning face against a lamp-post and cried, "I wish I could die."

When we were older Dad shared with us some of his experiences in the First World War, in which he and his younger brother George had both been signallers in the Navy. He told us about sailing in various convoys across the Atlantic to Galveston in the Gulf of Mexico, and how he and the other crew members enjoyed swimming in the warm sea of the Gulf, before setting off on the return voyage, hoping once again to survive the real dangers involved. At the end of one of these transatlantic trips he met up in Aden with his brother.

When George learned that Dad was due to set sail once more to Galveston, he said, "I would love to go there." When George informed Dad that he was due to sail back to Glasgow, Dad said, "If you want to go to the Naval office and see if we can switch ships, I am more than happy to return home to Glasgow." The naval authorities having no objection, they switched ships. Shortly after returning to Glasgow, my father's family were informed that George's ship had been blown up crossing the Atlantic. Dad never really got over that. It is a story I too have never forgotten, for had they not switched boats, I would not have been born.

In 1994 I was invited to conduct a special service in Edinburgh Castle to commemorate the 50th anniversary of the D-Day landings. It was a very moving occasion. So too was seeing my uncle George's name in the castle's Book of Remembrance.

Body Language

What people 'say' non-verbally is often more influential than what they say verbally. Body language is relevant in all aspects of our working life and social relationships, especially when communications involve an emotional element or when we meet someone for the first time. Body movements and facial expressions communicate thoughts, moods and attitudes – the pointing finger, the lover's frown, the child's pout, the parent's anxious look. They can indicate negative feelings such as disinterest, boredom and anxiety. We often learn more about what people are really thinking from the signals their bodies are broadcasting, than the words their mouths are uttering.

Our eyes are a significant aspect of the non-verbal signals we send to others. The cold phoney smile which is short-lived sends one message, the sunshine smile, creased up eyes, lips open and teeth in full view, communicates very different feelings. A quick raise of the eyebrow or folded arms, a blush or frown can indicate what a person is thinking and feeling without them uttering a word. A hand cupped round our ear says in effect, "I am having difficulty hearing you." Clasping someone's hand, or giving them a hug, can at a time of crisis express more powerfully than any words that we feel deeply for them. When in the company of someone whose opinions offend us, don't we find ourselves instinctively drawing back? Our body language says we want to dissociate ourselves from their views.

Sometimes, on television, a reporter's words are not synchronised with his or her gestures. Though this is sometimes amusing on the screen, it is not funny when in real life people's words are not synchronised with their facial expressions. We have all known children say 'Sorry' when their bodies and faces say something quite different. Sometimes after a heated discussion, a wife or husband will say, "Oh let us forget it", but the aggressive body language clearly indicates he or she does not intend to forget it. Our gestures constitute a language of their own.

When Words Fail

We named our black and white cat 'Boxer' because of the black circle round one of her eyes. Boxer regularly jumped on to my wife's lap, purring and vibrating in anticipation of having her back stroked and her chin scratched.

Children also have a deep-seated hunger for skin-touch. Henri Nouwen recalls an orphanage in Peru where the children, starved of affection, fought for the privilege of touching him. "These boys and girls only wanted one thing: to be touched, hugged, and caressed." How wonderful if every child could be guaranteed at least one good purring every day, if they had regular contact with people rich in caring love. The clasp of loving arms when thunder rolls, a pat on the head at bed-time, a kiss on a bruised knee – what comfort such touching can provide. The former Deputy Prime Minister, John Prescott, recently spoke of his life-long mistaken concept of masculinity. His great regret was that he had never hugged his sons.

Disturbed behaviour patterns in youngsters are often linked to sensory deprivation. Through the medium of touch, touch that has no sexual connotations, the beginning of a cure can often be set in motion. I have always had a warm feeling for the father of the prodigal son. He had every reason to be hurt by his younger son's irresponsible conduct. But when the lad returned home, the father did not wait at the door, or offer a reluctant handshake. He ran and fell on his son's neck and kissed him. By putting his arms round him he literally enfolded him with forgiveness.

Jesus took little children into his arms, put his hands upon them and blessed them. When a leper approached Jesus in desperation, Jesus did not simply utter a healing word from a safe distance. He stretched out his hand and touched him. Jesus felt deeply for lepers, cut off from all human contact. He touched untouchables.

The benefits of touch show up at every age. Touch can reduce pain, anxiety and depression. There are occasions when one can communicate far more through touch than words, times when no words are good enough or holy enough to minister to someone's pain. I recall receiving a phone-call one July morning from the captain of our 5th Glasgow Boys Brigade Company. He phoned to inform me that one of the boys had been killed in a road accident at the B.B. camp. Would I notify the boy's parents? There is no kind way of breaking such shattering news. The father understandably broke down. As he leaned forward, his head in his hands, I recall putting my hand on his sobbing head, and keeping it there for some time. His sobs gradually grew quieter. By means of touch I was able to communicate that my heart bled for him. Touch can be the very hand of God, the medium of divine comfort.

Response to touch seems to be the first response awakened in people, and the last to die. Premature babies who are held and touched, develop faster than those left alone. Old people need the loving touch of hands every bit as much as the young. Long after sight, hearing, speech and mental faculties are lost or impaired, the sense of touch remains. I recall an auxiliary in the geriatric hospital in Golspie, a middle-aged, over-worked, no-nonsense, but very caring person. The qualified nurses had far more medical knowledge, yet when Kathleen walked round the wards, trembling old arms were held out, and quivering voices often called 'Kathleen'. She treated each frail patient with the same respect as she would her own mother or grand-mother. Knowing the heart-hunger and skin-hunger of the old, Kathleen was lavish with her touch. She patted cheeks and gently pushed hair back from the forehead. Sometimes sensing a special need, she gave them a big hug.

Victor Hugo wrote of Bishop Bienvenu, "He understood how to sit down and hold his peace beside the man who had lost his wife, the mother who had lost her child. As he knew the moment for speech he also knew the moment for silence." He might well have added, 'and the moment for touch'.

Rabbi Harold Kushner entitled his best-seller, *When Bad Things Happen to Good People*, not *Why Bad Things Happen to Good People*. Because we are human we long to know why good people suffer from such life-threatening diseases as Cancer, Parkinson's, Multiple Sclerosis or Cystic Fibrosis, why crops rot with blight or lack of rain, why storms come and accidents happen. But just because we are only human we often cannot know.

A Madge Harrah tells how one afternoon she received a phone call from her mother to tell her that her brother and his wife and their two children had been killed in a car crash. Her mother begged her to come as soon as she could. While Madge's husband contacted neighbours and close friends and booked air flights, completely devastated by the news, she just stood, unable to focus her thoughts. Several friends phoned to say, "If there is anything we can do, let us know." She thanked them but was so traumatised, she could not think of anything. Just then the door bell rang. It was a neighbour who had heard about the crash. "I remember", he said, "when my father died suddenly, it took me a long time to get the children's shoes cleaned for the funeral. So that is what I have come to do. Give me all your shoes."

Madge was now faced with something specific to do. While the neighbour spread newspapers on the floor of the utility room, she gathered her own shoes and her husband's, and her children's very muddy shoes. The previous day on their way home from school, they had waded through mud. Watching him settle down and get to work on the shoes, helped her focus her own thoughts. She bathed the children and put them to bed. By the time she had finished, all their shoes, now spotless and gleaming, were lined up against the wall.

Some time later she wrote of that neighbour who had helped her find life on the other side of traumatic shock, "Now whenever I hear of someone who has lost a loved one, I no longer phone with the vague offer, 'If there is anything I can do, don't hesitate to let me know.' I try to think of one specific task that would help meet that person's need – offering to take the dog for a walk or to her home for a few days, or to do the ironing, or to look after the children the day of the funeral. When sometimes the person says to me, 'How did you know I needed that done?' I reply, 'Because a man once cleaned our shoes.'"

Many fine people know days like those experienced by Madge, when their heart is in pieces, when they wonder how it is possible that the sun continues to shine outside, and why the streets are still filled with cars, and why the world is still going about being the world, just as if nothing has happened. In such hours most people don't want letters or e-mails that attempt to explain the whys and wherefores of it all. What they want is someone who is willing to drop everything and come and make a coffee or a meal, or answer the telephone, and in a host of other ways stand beside them in their pain or disappointment. How invaluable are those who when life tumbles in, come to the rescue, people who only want to clean your shoes or hold your hand, people who simply bring food or flowers – the basics of beauty and life.

Good neighbours are not those who voice pious words when loss, loneliness or pain strikes, but those prepared to share the burden by hoisting it on to their own shoulders, who halve their neighbour's suffering and loneliness by taking it into their own heart, those willing to make time to listen. Doing the quiet unspectacular things that matter, precisely where we are, and with what we have, gives good neighbourliness its peculiarly resplendent quality.

Wise Words

Though George Washington Carver was born a slave, he became one of the greatest scientists of his day. For years he laboured to bring education to the black people of America. On one occasion Thomas Edison offered him a large salary if he would come and work with him. On hearing that he had turned down Edison's enticing offer, some of his contemporaries said, "Look, George, if you earned all that money, you could help your people." Aware of the frailties of human nature, Carver replied, "If I had all that money I might forget my people." On his tombstone are the words, "He could have added fame and fortune but cared for neither. He found happiness and honour in being helpful to the world."

The danger highlighted by George Carver is a real one. The Orkney poet George Mackay Brown wrote of an iron gate clanging behind those who have become absorbed in the world of getting and spending. Jesus warned his followers to "be on their guard against greed of every kind." The craving for more and more material possessions may be good for the economy. It just often happens not to be good for people. The absorbing struggle to become rich in material goods has caused many to lose their moral and spiritual bearings.

Using techniques our parents never dreamed of, advertisers seek to convince us that happiness depends on satisfying our longing for more and better things, an outlook denied by almost every religion and philosophy known to mankind. Tibetan Buddhists liken our endless craving for more, to a character called 'the hungry ghost'. This creature has an enormous stomach, but a small throat. Its appetite is never satisfied. What someone called 'Affluenza' has diverted many from exploring and enjoying the real wonder and glory of life and the world.

We live in a culture that honours celebrity status rather than worth, a culture where inflated salaries and bonuses are paid to egocentric footballers and pop stars, to top business executives and skinny models, a world on the other hand where teachers and nurses are undervalued and millions starve. I can think of people who financially did well in Scotland, but did not do well for Scotland. Emile Gauvreau wrote of middle-class society, "I was part of that strange race of people aptly described as spending their lives doing many things they don't really enjoy, buying things they don't need, to impress people they don't like." Many find themselves in considerable debt keeping up with friends who also are in considerable debt.

What disparity there often is between how we expend our everyday energies, and how we wish one day to be eulogised. Few would want the person who writes their obituary to highlight the size of the house lived in, or the luxury car they drove, or the fabulous holidays they enjoyed. And yet so many go on chasing things that in the long run do not accord with their deepest desires. "Getting and spending," said Wordsworth, "we lay waste our powers."

A group of people were one day discussing a man who because of an economic depression had fallen on hard times. When one lady remarked, "The savings of his lifetime have all been swept away," a wise old man said, "No, he may have lost his money, but he has retained his pleasure in living. He has made large investments in other lives. These have not depreciated, but are yielding a large return to society today." Then he added, "We don't have to worry about him. Let us rather worry about ourselves if the savings of our lifetime are such that they can all be swept away in an economic depression."

Discernment

It was another wise man who said that to every complex problem there is a simple solution. Then he added, "and that simple solution is usually wrong." A critic rightly said of William Morris' poem 'Love is Enough', "It is not." In the rough and tumble of everyday life something more is needed, the insight to determine priorities and grasp essentials, the ability to discern what is ultimately for the good of individuals and communities and what would ultimately be harmful. Without this there is the real danger of accepting our own preferences – what we feel inclined to do – and calling them by the grand words 'Christian Love'

How for example do you love the beggar who comes to your door and asks for money? That is not a simple question, not if you think of love in terms of seeking the highest good of the other person. In some cases to give money would be the worst possible thing to do. How does the judge love the criminal? How does he or she express concern for the person being tried, and also at the same time show a real concern for the individual or society that has been wronged? How do you show love to children whose lives are being warped by unreasonable parents? How does a married daughter love a demanding mother, without being unfair to her husband and family? There is no dictionary of conduct we can thumb through to find precise answers spelled out.

Just because the technical skill of the human race is immense, the possibilities for good and evil are also immense. Addressing a committee of M.P.s, Dr. Wilmut, who cloned Dolly the sheep, said concerning the possibility of cloning human beings, to which he personally is opposed, "If we really wanted to do it, it could be done." In an age of incredible technology, biological engineering and high-tech medicine, the burning question for many scientists and physicians is not so much "Can we do so and so?" but "Should we do so and so?" They need the gift of discernment.

Middle ways are never easy. Nor are they always fashionable with people who want to establish one pole as absolute truth, who think in terms of everything being black or white. Middle ways demand maturity. They demand discernment. Alongside scientific research and the enlargement of the frontiers of knowledge, there is a burning need for the pursuit of what the Bible calls wisdom, something larger and deeper than mere knowledge.

When Henry Sandon, of the 'Antique Roadshow', visited Dornoch with a B.B.C. crew to present a 'Songs of Praise' service from the Cathedral, I had to resist the temptation to take him to the antique shop opposite the

Cathedral, and get him to point out the real bargains! What I do remember is asking him how he acquired his ability to recognise and value rare pieces of porcelain. He told me he had learned it from others who loved beautiful porcelain. Is it not similar with the ability to discern wisely? Many of the wisest parents, teachers, politicians, and scientists I know acquired this ability from being a member of a home, church or community where the great truths and principles which Jesus stood for, treating other people as you would have them treat you, forgiving those who wrong us ... were highly valued, values and principles which are as relevant in our computer age as in agricultural Palestine.

Success – Failure

In response to the question, 'How do you measure success?' Ralph Waldo Emerson penned some wise words,

> *To laugh often and much*
> *To win the respect of intelligent people*
> *and the affection of children.*
> *To earn the appreciation of honest critics*
> *and endure the betrayal of false friends.*
> *To appreciate beauty*
> *To find the best in others*
> *To leave the world a bit better,*
> *whether by a redeemed social condition*
> *or a job well done*
> *– this is to have succeeded*

What strikes me about Emerson's definition is what he does not mention. There is absolutely no mention of wealth or health, celebrity status or having power over others.

Failure, as the world conceives it, is a word found not only in the dictionary of fools and cowards, but of many outstanding people. Addressing students at St. Andrews University, J. M. Barrie, the author of *Peter Pan*, reminded them that "We are all failures – at least the best of us are." Think of the delight Mozart has brought to thousands, how his music has enriched the world. And yet Mozart died in abject poverty. In the 19th century Father Damien cast in his lot with the leper community on the island of Molokai. He became the physician of their souls and bodies, their teacher, carpenter, gardener, cook and even grave-digger. After twelve strenuous years Damien himself contracted and died of the dreaded disease, leaving few worldly possessions. Was Damien a failure? The Belgian people did not think so. A few years ago they voted him the greatest Belgian of all time.

After-Dinner Speaking

I sometimes think Britain has become the dinner capital of the world. Every profession, institution, rugby club, golf club, rotary and probus club has its annual dinner. Countless charities have fund-raising lunches. Waitresses squeeze through tiny gaps between the tables, often to serve hundreds of guests. Some attend such lunches and dinners to enjoy what the speakers have to say, but there are also often a few who are just waiting to be critical. If they agree with the speakers they are deemed to be fine orators. If they disagree with them they are windbags. Whether an after-dinner speech is good or bad depends, however, not just on the speaker, but also the audience.

The distinguished American politician Adlai Stevenson once said to the audience he was addressing, "I am going to start speaking and you are going to start listening. I hope we will both stop at the same time." That is the hope of every public speaker. You quickly learn that if in the first few minutes you don't get a half-nelson on your audience, you have lost them forever.

The late Sir Nicholas Fairbairn, a former M.P for Perthshire, told of a Highlander who sought to explain why he always followed his nip of whisky with a beer: "If you just drink whisky you get tight before you are full, and if you just drink beer, you get full before you are tight, but if you drink them together you get full and tight at the same time, and you know when to stop." Unfortunately some who attend dinners don't know when they have had enough. Though *Slainte* (slange) is a Scots term for health, some seem to think it means, "slam the drink down your throat and have another one."

I will never forget being invited to propose the toast to the St Andrew's Society of Belfast. Firms who had invited guests, mainly business clients, had put bottles of wine and whiskey on the tables. When these were emptied, fresh bottles were provided. I was fort-unate in being the first to speak when the majority of the guests were still reasonably sober. I was followed by a High Court judge who was incredibly boring. As I listened to him I was reminded of the reply Churchill once gave to a politician, who after delivering a speech, asked Churchill how he could put more fire into his speeches. "Your problem," said a very blunt Churchill, "was not lack of fire in your speech, but that you did not put that speech into the fire." So should the Judge have done that night. As he went on and on, many who had given up listening, consumed more and more of the free alcohol. By eleven o'clock, over-worked livers were howling in protest.

My heart bled for the final speaker – a delightful man, Dr. Johnnie Kyle, one of Ireland's legendary rugby players. Though he was an excellent speaker, many by that time were not listening. When one man fell off his chair, I was reminded of a story of Peter Ustinov's. He told how he stayed one night at a hotel noted for its frequent Freemason functions. When he was asked in the morning if he had slept well, he replied, "Afraid not. A party raged all night and the hotel resounded to the sound of falling masonry!" Excessive drinking on the part of a few can ruin a dinner. Sometimes those who have reached the stage of being 'past the pint of no return' start heckling. That can make after-dinner speaking a real lottery.

Having said that, the sober witty heckler can sometimes add to the evening. John Cole, the highly regarded political commentator, who hailed from Belfast, told of a dinner he once attended. The rather pompous chairman began the evening's proceedings by delivering a lengthy grace in Latin. The slight tittering when he ended, burst into loud laughter when one of the guests was heard to say, "That takes us back a few centuries."

I love the story, even though it may be apocryphal, of how when a Rabbi in an after dinner speech used Moses as an example of great leadership, a Jewish gentleman in the audience interrupted him, "Moses was not a good leader." Ignoring the interruption the rabbi continued. A little later the man shouted out again, "Moses was a very poor leader." This time the rabbi stopped and asked the heckler why he was profaning the memory of such an outstanding leader. "Well," said the man, "for forty years he kept the children of Israel in the desert, before bringing them to the only Middle East country without oil."

Wedding speeches

Some speakers at wedding dinners go through hell for days before they have to speak. Many a bride's father, bridegroom and best man have visibly trembled as I called on them to speak. For them, the starter and roast beef had come and gone in a haze. The portions placed in front of them were taken away virtually untouched. When they did finally rise to speak, the faces in the audience were like cardboard cut-outs. At one unforgettable wedding, all three speakers, beginning with the bride's father, completely froze when they stood up. Their minds went blank. Not one of them had taken the trouble to write anything down. At that wedding I finished up not only proposing the toast to the bride and groom, but replying on behalf of the bridegroom and proposing the toast to the bridesmaids.

In the early 1970s a Glasgow minister told me of an even more unusual wedding and after-dinner speeches. Denny Grieve was a delightful but very traditional kirk minister. He regularly dressed in a dark striped suit and dark raincoat. For several years his neighbour in Kelvinside was the comedian Billy Connolly. When Denny one day said to me that he sometimes felt that when Billy Connolly portrayed a church minister, he was really portraying him, I did not know what to say, for that same thought had crossed my mind. One Saturday morning Denny was wakened at eight o'clock by the doorbell ringing. Standing on the doorstep was a young man with an older woman. Though still in his dressing gown, he invited them in. Only then did it dawn on him that the young man was the bridegroom whose wedding ceremony he was due to conduct that afternoon. When he inquired how he could help, the older lady explained that her daughter, the bride to be, had had a baby prematurely in Rottenrow Hospital during the night. (Rotten Row is a corruption of '*route du roi*' – the King's Way.) The bridegroom wondered if he would marry them in the hospital. Mr. Grieve explained that this would depend on the Registrar being willing to issue a new marriage certificate listing the new place of marriage. Fortunately the Registrar was cooperative. Having married them later that morning in a side room in the hospital, Denny then went on to the church to inform the guests that the wedding had taken place, but that the wedding reception would go on as planned. At the reception he acted as chairman, as was customary in these days. He watched carefully everything he said, for never before had he been present at a wedding at which the bride was not present. All went reasonably well until, after the bride's father, best man and bridegroom had said a very few words, a guest rose and said he would like to propose a toast to absent friends!

A difficult art

Though accomplished speakers often make the art of public speaking appear easy, it is anything but easy. When a reporter asked the elderly Churchill what things he found most difficult, he replied, "Climbing a ladder leaning towards me, kissing a girl leaning away from me, and giving an after-dinner speech!" When Archbishop Fulton Sheen, one of America's finest broadcasters and after-dinner speakers, was asked the secret of his obvious mastery of the art, he said it was, "Ten percent delivery and ninety percent thinking, study, sweat and hard work."

When Willie Allan, an accomplished Scottish after-dinner speaker, rises to his feet, there is no sweat on his forehead, no wavering in his voice, as he tells his audience how when Bonnie Prince Charlie died, he was first buried in a dry-stone dyke. For proof of this relatively unknown fact, he quoted the well-known song "Bonnie Charlie's noo a wa'."

Then with impeccable timing he went on to tell his audience how the Prince's remains were later removed from the wall and given a proper burial. As proof of this, he quoted another line from a Scots song, "He's no a wa' tae bide a wa'."!! Willie Allan has such a wonderful way of telling these absurd stories that the audience laughs heartily.

What one person finds hilarious, others do not. Pam Ayers, a brilliant humorous wordsmith, tells of writing what she thought was a humorous letter to her manager, called Mr. Branch. In her letter she used many tree-related words. She spoke of the danger of barking up the wrong tree, of the need to get to the root of office problems, to cut out the dead wood, and get the staff to turn over a new leaf. Her boss was not amused. Thereafter they had strained relationships.

I much prefer speaking to a mixed audience, for I find off-putting the kind of jokes which too often are the main diet at all-male dinners. Some speakers seem to think that their speech would be insipid unless salted by swear words and sexual innuendos. How mistaken they are. Though they may gain a few cheap laughs, they do not win the respect of the majority of those present.

At a London dinner the chairman noticed a news photographer jockeying for a vantage point for an action shot of the main speaker – a leading politician. Fearing that the speaker might be upset by the flash going off, the chairman called the photographer and said, "Don't take his picture while he is speaking. Shoot him before he starts." I can think of some speakers whom I wish had been shot before they started.

Introductions

The cricketer Freddie Truman told how he was once invited to be the guest speaker at a dinner. Before he rose to speak, the chairman whispered, "Keep it short. Remember we are here to enjoy ourselves." Just as speakers vary in quality, so do the introductions they receive. The aim of a good chairperson is by their introduction to open the door between the speaker and his or her audience. Some open the door beautifully, whetting the audience's appetite. But others stand in the doorway far too long, sometimes so long that the speaker's greatest problem is wakening up the audience. I remember once thanking a very long-winded chairman for his words of introduction. I said, not all that sincerely, that I could have listened to such an introduction all night. What I was tempted to add was, "and for a few moments I thought I was going to have to". But I refrained.

During my year as Moderator of the Church of Scotland, I was invited to speak at a dinner in Glasgow at which Eddie George, the former Governor of the Bank of England, was the other speaker. After Mr. George had given his account of the economic state of

Britain, the chairman introduced me by saying "We were awfully glad when Dr. Simpson was nominated as Moderator, for we were getting awfully tired of these intellectuals!" On yet another occasion a lady president said, "There is really no need for me to introduce Dr. Simpson for I am sure you all know him in one way or another, through his preaching or books." So far, so good, but then she continued, "I have never known a minister who can hold me as Dr. Simpson does."

A chairman once had the task of explaining to a large banquet audience what he called a slight hitch in the proceedings. "Ladies and Gentlemen," he intoned, "the guest of honour this evening needs no introduction – he has not turned up!"

After a very elaborate introduction lauding the guest speaker as an industrial giant, the speaker began by admitting that all the chairman had said about him was true. "I did start work as the messenger boy, bringing my lunch in a paper bag. I did work my way up from one department to another. At the age of thirty-two I was elected chairman of the company. Your chairman just omitted one thing. He failed to inform you that my father owns the company."

The preference of most speakers is when the chairman does not overdo the introductory hymn of praise. I remember once thinking as I listened to the chairman's over-the-top flattering remarks, I now know how a plum pudding must feel after it has had treacle poured all over it. Slowly rising to his feet after a very detailed introduction, one speaker said that the only detail the chairman had omitted to mention was that he had been born by Caesarean section. Then he added,

"That explains why I sometimes like to leave houses by the window instead of the front door."

Sometimes, at very formal dinners, speakers are introduced by a specially hired Master of Ceremonies. Though immaculately attired in red jacket and bow-tie, such toastmasters don't always get things right. Sir Lionel Luckhoo tells how when he was High Commissioner for Guyana and Barbados, he was invited to be the principal speaker at a House of Commons dinner. When it was his turn to speak the M.C. instead of saying, "Pray silence for ..." said, "Pray for the silence of His Excellency the High Commissioner." Rising to his feet Sir Lionel said, "My Lords, ladies and gentlemen, your prayers are answered." To deafening cheers he sat down. He did however rise a few seconds later.

Probably the most famous case of a lengthy introduction was when at a London dinner the chairman droned on interminably in introducing the playwright George Bernard Shaw. When after thirty minutes he finally sat down, Shaw slowly rose to his feet and said, "Ladies and gentlemen, the subject is not exhausted but we are." I am told he then sat down, and did not rise again.

Good medicine

Most people don't come to a dinner to be educated or bored. They come to be entertained. It was because laughter is a helpful aid to digestion, that our ancestors arranged for jesters to be present at banquets. I sometimes wonder if after dinner speakers are their modern equivalent? When Jack Milroy, the brilliant comedian and after-dinner speaker died, it was said of him, "He was a walking national health service. He dispensed more good than some chemists." Kindly laughter is good medicine.

Self-deprecating humour can enrich a speech. Kenneth Galbraith enjoyed telling audiences his wife's comment on the lengthiness of his speeches: "She says that people may not be a great deal wiser after my talks, but they are often a great deal older." I remember at one dinner the main speaker, who was not the most handsome of men, began by telling his audience how as a boy he had been so plain looking, that the first time he played hide and seek, nobody came looking for him! That endeared him to the audience. At a function where the majority of the audience were psychiatrists, the actor John Cleese of 'Fawlty Towers' fame introduced himself as Britain's best known psychiatric patient! The American comedian Rodney Dangerfield told at another dinner how a psychiatrist once informed him that he was crazy. Upset on hearing this, he told the psychiatrist he wanted a second opinion. "All right," he said, "You are ugly too."

A judge once used the language of the law-courts to shed light on the art of after-dinner speaking. "You must have an arresting beginning, a few appropriate sentences for the middle, and a brief ending. You must also speak with conviction." Good advice. A blend of seriousness, and humour that is relevant to the occasion, can also enrich a speech.

I have attended dinners where some speakers have simply told one joke after another, many of which really had little or no bearing on the occasion. Listening to such a speech is like eating cookies that are nothing but chocolate chips. It does not take long for your teeth to begin aching. I personally long for something more substantial. For me wit is the salt of an after dinner speech, not the food.

When Irvin S. Cobb, having spoken at great length at a dinner, finally sat down, the chairman said, "Ladies and gentlemen, you have just been listening to the ancient Chinese sage, On Too Long!" Having listened at dinners to some of On Too Long's close relations, I am convinced the greatest secret of being a successful public speaker is stopping talking before your audience stops listening.

A Lump in Our Throats

When shortly after his daughter's death, King Lear realised all that Cordelia had sacrificed for him, he said, "Upon such sacrifices the gods themselves throw incense." There was a lump in his throat and tears in his eyes as the old king spoke.

When the Nazis were liquidating Jews and the mentally ill, one distraught mother refused to part with her baby. Without a word, a nun called Mother Maria pushed the baby's mother aside and quietly took her place. Fortunately the officer in charge that day was only interested in the correct numerical returns. Not surprisingly there was a lump in the throat and tears in the eyes of many who watched as the nun walked quietly to her death. They sensed they were standing on holy ground.

One of the first to speak out strongly against war was the Greek writer Euripides. In his drama, *The Trojan Women*, he depicted war, not in terms of a soldier armed to the teeth, bristling with courage and armour, but in terms of a woman with a dead baby in her arms. He thus reminded his contemporaries that war is not simply grown-ups slaying other grown-ups, but the maiming and destruction of the minds and bodies of countless children.

I have never forgotten watching on television, President Sadat of Egypt being welcomed in Jerusalem by the Israeli Prime Minister, Golda Meir. Sadat had flown from Cairo for an historic meeting between Arab and Jewish leaders. Now it so happened that Sadat's first grandchild was born the day before he left Cairo. In her words of welcome Golda Meir said to Sadat, "I have been a grandmother for some years. Let me give you a gift for your new grandchild." Sadat's chin trembled as he accepted the gift. A lump rose in his throat, and I am sure in the throats of many viewers. For a moment we glimpsed how much finer this world would be if only the leaders of the nations, Arab and Jew, Sunni and Shi'a, Tutsi and Hutu, Westerners and Taliban, were to love their children and grandchildren more and hate their enemies less.

The real horror of war and terrorism is seen in what it does to children. Whereas for centuries, even as late as the First World War, the vast majority who died in war were professional soldiers, in more recent times the vast majority who die are civilians. Many won't quickly forget the tragic pictures from Syria of orphaned babies and severely wounded children, or the pictures of dead children being dug out of the rubble and carried away in black bags, or the sobbing picture of an Iraqi child whose mother had been killed by a suicide bomber. Seeing grown-ups suffer is bad enough, but children, shocked and scared, longing for their dead Mum's embrace, that is different. They don't know what it is all about.

After the defeat of Napoleon, the Russian and Austrian armies sought vengeance. In one Italian village the women fled to the church for safety, but the soldiers followed and brutally slew them. One mother escaped by hiding her infant son in the church belfry. That infant was to become the brilliant composer Verdi. How much poorer the world would have been if that child had also been slaughtered, if he had not been able to enrich the world with his *Rigoletto*, *Aida* and *La Traviata*. When children become the jury, terrorism and war are seen to be the destructive and horrific things they really are. I wonder if in our day a future Verdi was among the children slaughtered in Iraq or Syria, or a future Einstein in the Palestinian-Israeli conflicts.

When we set a child in the midst we see not only the horror of war, but the horror of human greed and apathy. The historical records which describe the awful conditions under which many children had to work in the 19th century in the factories and mines, make heart-rending reading. Children under nine often had to work twelve hours a day. Many members of Britain's ruling classes saw nothing wrong in this. Today we look back and wonder how people could have been so blind and heartless.

I cannot help thinking that a hundred years from now, our descendants may look back and wonder at how in the 21st century one quarter of the world's population could be so indifferent to the appalling needs of the other three quarters. Could a future Nelson Mandela have been among those who have died of starvation in Africa this past decade?

Poetic Words

The magic of great poetry lies in its power to compress ideas and emotions into a handful of words. Great poets have helped many, including myself, better hear, see and understand. Perhaps it is because of my early scientific training, with its emphasis on technical journals and literature of the textbook kind, where words and ideas were defined with great precision, that I often struggle with modern poetry. I become impatient with its lack of form and rhyme, its lack of precision and clarity, and sometimes its verbal foliage.

At a time when poetry in the English speaking world is largely written for other poets, and for a tiny minority of the general public, there is something heartening in the fact that Robert Burns is still so highly regarded. There have been more intellectual poets, but few have had Burns' ability to express in simple words the feelings of ordinary folk.

Burns wrote, "My muse tho' hamely in attire, may touch the heart." Burns' hamely poetry not only came from the heart, it touched many hearts. Midnight oil may have been burnt in writing his poems, but you never catch the smell of it.

Had we never loved sae kindly!
Had we never loved sae blindly!
Never met – or never parted,
We had ne'er been broken-hearted.

What magnificent simplicity. His poem about a farmer's New Year greeting to his old mare, and his poems about a mouse and a mountain daisy, are equally simple. His love poems, almost three hundred of them, have touched the hearts of people in every continent.

More than a hundred years ago, an American, Robert Ingersoll, after visiting Burns' birthplace in Alloway, penned these very moving words

Though Scotland boasts a thousand names
of patriot, king and peer,
The noblest, grandest of them all
was loved and cradled here.
Here lived the gentle peasant prince,
the loving cottar king
Compared with whom the greatest Lord
is but a titled thing.

'Tis but a cot roofed in with straw,
a hovel made of clay.
One door shuts out the wind and storms —
one window greets the day.
And yet I stand within this room
and hold all thrones in scorn,
For here beneath this lowly thatch,
Love's sweetest bard was born.

At one stage in his life Burns doubted the worthwhileness of being a poet. He felt he would have been better off had he worked in a bank.

I backward mus'd on wasted time
How I had spent my youthfu' prime
An' done nae-thing
But stringing blethers up in rhyme
For fools to sing.

Had I to guid advice but harkit
I might, by this, hae led a market
Or strutted in a bank...

In this poem, 'The Vision', Burns tells us how in his lowly cottage he had one day a vision of an attractive Muse entering, a Muse who reminded him of the contribution he was making as a poet to Scottish life. The Muse finishes with these words.

Then never murmur nor repine;
Strive in thy humble sphere to shine;
And trust me, not Potosi's mine,
Nor king's regard,
Can give a bliss o'ermatching thine,
A rustic bard.

I am glad I was introduced at an early age to Burns' poetry. What insights he provides into human emotions.

For me equally moving and insightful was a recent poem by Lucy Berry entitled 'Out of a Copper Mine'. The poem which I heard read on the radio was about the Chilean miners who were entombed for several weeks. In her simple but profound poem she highlights the importance of those everyday things which the buried miners had long taken for granted, until they realised they might never enjoy them again. In their underground prison they underwent a transvaluation of the world's values. Commonplace things like light and fresh air, like love of family and friends, soared from the bottom to the top of their priority lists.

When the whole world shifts and creaks
in the press of rock above you;
and there are no doors from the night
to the ones who love you

(and the silly bright metal you prized
and the zeal with which you mined it,
is part of the dark, and the dark,
and the dark of eyes blinded)...

you yearn for the sameness of light.
And a breeze. And your parents' faces.
And the kiss of a loving child.
And your wife's embraces

and hailing a friend on the street
as if there was nothing to it;
the ordinary things which are blessed
though you never knew it.

And long after you have been freed
from that outer and inner night
as an old, old man you'll recall
your first new glimpse of the sight
of human faces and hands
and the blessed greatness of Light.

The habit of looking at things as if we were seeing
them for the last time, and doing little commonplace
things finely has given many a better quality of life.
Imagine we will never again experience the delight of
having a meal with those we dearly love and value, or
the enjoyment of a warm piece of buttered toast in the
morning, or the excitement of a good book, or the
welcoming wagging tail of a dog, or salt-laden air at the
beach, or a glorious sunset, or a full moon hanging in a

black starry sky on a frosty night, or a beautiful flower garden, or a majestic mountain scene, or the glimpse of a red-tailed hawk circling above, or the great variety of bird song. Cultivating that habit could well help us master what for some people is the hardest arithmetic – that which enables them to count their blessings.

Long may such poetry continue to be written.

When the Word Became Flesh (Christmas)

Nativity Plays

Judi Dench tells how one December her daughter returned from school very excited. She informed her mother that their infant class was putting on a play. When Judi asked what it was about, she said, "It is about an inn-keeper's wife" "Oh," said Judi, slightly surprised, "And do you have a part in the play?" "Yes Mummy, I am the inn-keeper's wife." Her daughter was convinced that the main character in the play was not Mary or Joseph or the baby Jesus, but the inn-keeper's wife!

What fond memories I have of nativity plays, of awe-struck toddlers dressed in coloured dressing gowns or angel costumes being herded down church aisles. From beside the Christmas tree or a bale of straw, they wave to their proud parents and grandparents. Who does not feel a lump in their throat or experience a tear trickling down their cheek as the children sing, 'Away in a manger', even if sometimes the words are unwittingly amended: "A wean in a manger no crib for a bed, the little Lord Jesus laid down his wee Ted"?

Many unplanned and humorous things happen in nativity plays. For years thereafter families recall the night little Jimmy got hit by a shepherd's crook and ran screaming down the aisle to his parents, or how one of the angels fell off her pedestal, or how little Jean effectively eclipsed the rest of the choir as she belted out, 'Twinkle, twinkle little star'.

A London teacher, who had the responsibility of producing the school's nativity play, tells how in spite of much coaching, she was sure that on the big night some of the children would forget their lines. It duly happened. At one point in the performance, Mary and Joseph, both aged eleven, stood for some time in helpless silence, broken finally by Mary stepping forward and thumping Joseph. "Wyke up Joe. I fink I'm goin' to 'ave a byeby." Joseph's reaction to the news was less than enthusiastic. "Cor. Whatever next?"

A decade ago it was the in thing to tell children the Christmas story and then let the youngsters express the story in their own words – sometimes with unexpected consequences! I think of the inn-keeper who, having told Joseph that there was no room in the inn, then quickly added, "But come away in for a drink." In a televised nativity play from a Paisley school the narrator lisped the Christmas story in her own words. "Jesus was born in the middle of the night, and Mary and Joseph woke up to see what was happening." I am sure Mary wished her baby's birth had been that easy. A second narrator then added, "And that is why we sellotape Christmas."

A few years ago a friend's grandson was involved in a nativity play. Instead of saying as he was meant to, "And an angel did appear in the sky," he said, to his parents' embarrassment, but to the great amusement of the audience, "And an angel did a pee in the sky."

Many have fond memories of nativity plays in which they took part. Not so, however, a woman interviewed on the radio. When she was a little girl, her teacher, a Miss Stringer, about whom she still has occasional nightmares, would not let her be an angel in the school nativity play. "Angels don't wear glasses," she said firmly. When finally cast as an ox, she muttered to her friend that she had never seen an ox with glasses! Unfortunately Miss Stringer heard her and made her write out a hundred times, "I must not talk back to the teacher." Poor wee soul!

Nativity plays help swell audiences and congregations, but far more important they give young people a feel for the greatest love story ever told, the story of how "God so loved the world that he gave his only son."

Scrooge

The novels of Charles Dickens, like those of Tolstoy and Dostoevsky, have taught me more about human behaviour than many psychological and theological textbooks. Though *A Christmas Carol* is not a religious book, the re-reading of it recently was for me a religious experience. I believe one of the reasons it has stayed alive for more than 160 years is that in most of us there is the desire to be a better person, to know a deeper joy, to become more fully human. Dickens' fictional story sheds more light on the real meaning of 'conversion' and 'redemption' than many a sermon I have heard. It highlights the good news of the Gospel that people can be brought to think differently and act differently,

The central character is a 'squeezing, wrenching, grasping, scraping, clutching, covetous old sinner'. For Scrooge, Christmas was humbug: "If I could work my will, every idiot who goes about with 'Merry Christmas' on his lips would be boiled in his own Christmas pudding, and buried with a stake of holly through his heart." The change in Scrooge takes place in clearly marked stages. While sitting in his gloomy lodgings there appeared the ghost of his former partner Jacob Marley, who had been almost as mean as Scrooge. Marley's mission was to save Scrooge from the fate he had suffered by getting him to take a critical look at his way of life. "I wear the chain I forged in life," explained Marley, "I made it link by link." "But," said Scrooge, "you were always a good man of business." "Business," said Marley, "the common welfare should have been my business ... Why did I walk through crowds of fellow human beings with my eyes turned down and never raised to that blessed star which led the Wise Men to a poor abode? Were there no poor homes to which its light would have conducted me?" Before Marley's ghost left, he told Scrooge he would be visited by three spirits.

The first was that of Christmas past, Scrooge's past. Scrooge was treated to what we would call 'flashbacks' of the Christmases of his childhood. He was reminded of Christmas at the home of Mr Fezziwig, a bright happy man for whom Scrooge used to work. He was also reminded of the girl he did not marry because his love of money had displaced her as the object of his affection. He glimpsed young Belle, now happily married to another. During these flashbacks, Scrooge keeps muttering, "I wish ... but it is too late now."

Dickens knew that memory has a way of opening us up, a way of posing the question, "Have we paid too much for what we have achieved or amassed?"

The second spirit to visit Scrooge was that of Christmas present. He is taken to the modest house of his clerk Bob Cratchit. There was more joy in that house than Scrooge had ever known. The scene made a deep impression on Scrooge. It has made a deep impression on many since. It can be disconcerting to see others derive so much joy from so little, while we experience little real happiness with so much. Addressing graduating students at McGill University, Rudyard Kipling warned them against becoming too preoccupied with fame and wealth: "Some day you will meet a person who cares for none of these things, and then you will know how poor you are."

The third spirit gave Scrooge a preview of the future, the tomorrow being fashioned out of his todays. He was taken round the town's business centre. There his fellow-businessmen were casually discussing a death – his death. It was obvious they felt no real sense of loss. He was then shown a shop where three unattractive characters were pawning possessions that had been taken from the dead person's home. No one seemed to care. For Scrooge this was another moment of truth. "I see, I see." Then he asks in desperation, "Are these the shadows of the things that will be, or are they the shadows of the things that may only be?" A ray of hope breaks in as he asks this question.

The third ghost succeeded in getting Scrooge to contemplate the overall effect of his life. As a result of his journeys into the past, present and future, Scrooge changed. He woke up from his nightmare grateful to be alive. He went up and down the streets wishing everyone a Merry Christmas. He went to church. He bought a huge turkey and sent it to the Cratchit home. He raised Bob Cratchit's salary. He became like a second father to Tiny Tim. "He became as good a master, and as good a man as the good old city knew."

Some will say, "Ah, but it is only fiction." Personally I believe it is more than that. It is a parable of the change for the better that has been wrought in many lives. Three things changed Scrooge.

1. He was brought to think seriously about his ways. How often it is during such moments that God holds his most serious conversations with us.

2. Scrooge realised that despite the unlikeable person he was, he was still loved. Even when no one else could stand him, Bob Cratchit continued to see worth in him.

3. Scrooge realised he was needed. If he got with it, Tiny Tim might yet live.

Dickens' classic story is for me a powerful reminder that what matters most is not whether we have fallen, but whether we will get up. More important than whom we have hurt in the past, is who we will help in the future.

The Muffled Presence of the Holy

An old legend of the Western Isles tells of a sea-king who longed for the company of a human being. One day in his cavern under the sea, he heard a little human cry. Rising to the surface he discovered a child in a derelict boat. As he was about to reach the vessel and take the child, a rescue party intervened. According to the legend, as they sailed away, the sea-king cupped his hands and threw a little sea-salt wave into the heart of the child. As he submerged, he said, "The child is mine. When he grows, the salt sea will call him and he will come home to me at the last." It is only a Gaelic legend, but like many legends, it enshrines timeless truths.

A hundred and fifty years ago in the ranches of America, there were rough, tough men who were cradled in the glens of Scotland. You might live with them for months and never learn that they remembered home. But then one evening there would come the strain of Scottish music, some highland lilt, and on that restless company there would fall a quietness. Some were seen wiping tears from their eyes. Then it took no prophet to discover that the thirst for their homeland was not dead.

The majority of us drift along on the surface of life. We avoid long thoughts. We will talk about anything except our hidden origin and destiny, and what is going on beneath the surface in our minds and lives. But sometimes even those whom the whole subject of religion leaves cold, are hushed and startled to find their hearts leaping and their eyes misting over, perhaps on holding a newborn child or grandchild, or glimpsing a frail elderly person struggling to put food on a bird table on a freezing cold December day, or hearing a Salvation Army band playing a familiar carol in the street. Something within them also resonates when they read of someone like Oskar Schindler risking his life to save Jews from the holocaust. I suspect many so-called atheists are not as atheistic as they think. In Camus' novel *The Plague* a surprising, but very moving conversation takes place between two atheists. "What interests me," says one, "is learning to become a saint."

Beneath the yearning for what glitters brightest, and the greed that longs to sit on full moneybags, there is often a sense of emptiness, unease and incompleteness, a hunger for more than food, a thirst for more than drink, a longing for a joy deeper than the good times and bad times life metes out, and a feeling that we were made to live with hands, not clenched to grasp, but stretched out to share and receive with joy. Though like Adam and Eve many have lost Paradise, they still carry something of Paradise around inside them, a latent yearning to become more fully alive, more fully human.

On Christmas Eve some, who throughout the year are not 'kirk greedy', wend their way to church. I believe many of them do so, not simply because of the novelty of the hour, but because deep down, in the story of him who was born at Christmas, they sense the muffled presence of the holy. It is impossible to conceive how different the history of art, music, literature, our culture and political institutions, and our understanding of ourselves, would have been had Jesus not been born. Such was the magnetism, intellectual power and compassion of Jesus, that men folded their nets, beached their boats and went with him. Two thousand years later, the life he lived, the truths he taught, the values for which he stood, continue to strike responsive chords in the hearts of many.

Three Life-Enriching Words

Hope

A teacher who worked in a large hospital tells how a colleague from a nearby school contacted her about a pupil who had been admitted to hospital. She hoped she would visit the young lad and help him with his schoolwork. She explained that the class were at present studying adverbs. On arriving at the ward, the hospital teacher was dismayed to find that the lad was seriously ill. She told him that his teacher had asked her to do adverbs with him. Though embarrassed at putting such an ill child through what she thought was an unimportant exercise, she spoke for ten minutes about how adverbs add meaning to verbs.

The following morning the nursing sister said to her, "What did you do to that boy yesterday?" Before the teacher could get out her apology, the nurse said, "We had almost given up on him, but ever since you visited him, he seems to be fighting back and responding better to his treatment." The boy later explained that he had given up hope of getting better, but it all changed when he realised that they would not send someone to teach grammar to a dying boy, would they?

The power of hope! A painting entitled 'Hope' depicts a woman playing an instrument which had obviously once had several strings, but all except one were broken. Using the only string left, she was making what music she could. What a remarkable thing hope is, what an ally for example in the world of medicine, the hope that soon a cure will be found, or a transplant provide a new lease of life. When on television I see refugees leaving devastated homes with their few belongings, I marvel that they are travelling at all, and not just sitting down in despair.

It is reckoned that a child falls about four hundred times in learning to walk. Imagine if a despairing child said, "It is not worth trying to get up again." How life would be impoverished. Admittedly it is hard at times not to buckle to a feeling of despair in a world like ours. It is hard to keep getting up when knocked down, to keep putting one foot in front of the other, to go on hoping against the odds. Barack Obama could have cursed the early break-up of his parents' marriage. He could also, in his early working years in a tough Chicago community, have given up in his attempts to improve health care and job training and to counteract drug abuse, when he was faced with fierce resistance. But instead he kept on challenging the odds in an attempt to improve conditions in Altgeld. The title of his book, *The Audacity of Hope*, expresses the President's strong belief that we can help make things better. Whereas shallow optimism is a passive virtue, hope is an active one. Whereas optimism is the belief that things are changing for the better; hope is the belief that together we can make things better. Whereas despair readily gives up on problems, convinced they are bound to get worse, hope arouses our minds to explore every possibility of combating them. Hope keeps us dreaming, striving to lift things to a new level, even when there appears to be little to build on.

To be an agent of hope is a high calling.

Encouragement

To give young people the feeling that what they do, the words they speak, the kindnesses they show, matter a great deal, is about the finest thing we can do for them.

Charlie Chaplin's father was a struggling entertainer. His excessive drinking led to the break-up of his marriage when Charlie was only three years of age. Thereafter his mother had to move from one miserable apartment to another. In his autobiography Charlie pays his mother a tremendous compliment. He says that, despite their poor quarters, she made all her children feel they were important, and that they could make a worthwhile contribution to the life of the world. His father had lacked this assurance. Like many in our day he drank his life away because he felt it was of no significance anyway. Though some people have an over-inflated opinion of their importance, many more have too low an opinion. Most bullies and braggarts lack a sense of real worth.

They have never known the warm feeling of being told they are important or of being made to feel important. For a long time schools were so organised that the not so clever and less athletic youngsters were given the impression that they were not as important as those who shone in exams or on the sports field. Marking methods evaluated and recorded their weaknesses, not their strengths.

If we were able to probe people's inmost thoughts, I am sure we would often hear the cry, "I want to be a somebody, not a nobody." The great enemy of life is not pain or disease or physical hardship, but the feeling that we are not important, that what we do does not ultimately matter. How often a word of encouragement at the right time has been the turning point in struggling or aimless lives. It has helped undergird their resolve to do what they can as well as they can, and sometimes to take a stand for what they believe is right. "Keep up the good work, Fred." "All power to your elbow, Jean." Such encouraging words, which cost nothing but a moment's thought and effort, can help people rise above mediocrity.

An elderly Quaker woman was once introduced to Abraham Lincoln. Shaking hands with the President, she uttered some sincere words of approval for what he was doing to abolish injustice and slavery. With a tear in his eye, Lincoln thanked the old lady: "You have given a cup of cold water to a very thirsty man." For Lincoln it was a grim battle. Daily maligned by those with a vested interest in the slave trade, he must occasionally have been tempted to ask, "Is it worth it?" A word of praise and encouragement refreshed him for the struggle. There are few ministries more important than the ministry of encouragement.

Acceptance

A Glasgow police inspector told me of a midnight car chase. The car in front kept swerving to prevent them overtaking. When they finally succeeded in halting the car, they found inside two thirteen-year-old boys and a load of stolen goods. "Right bad boys," we are tempted to say. But that is only half the story. When he called at their homes to inform the parents, he discovered the boys had been away from home for four days. The parents had not even reported them missing.

At a camp held many years ago at Aultbea in Wester Ross, boys from a young offenders' institution were each given the responsibility of looking after a special needs youngster. At the end of a day's climbing, one of the Borstal boys was found sobbing. The leader later learned, that on returning to camp, the Down-Syndrome youngster, whom the lad had helped, and with whom he had shared lunch, had come and sat on his knee, put his arms round him and said, "I love you." No one had ever said that to him before!

The greatest need of most disruptive and troubled youngsters is to be brought into contact with someone – a teacher, youth leader, friend or minister who takes a genuine interest in them, who restores their sense of worth by convincing them they count for something. Jimmy Boyle, who came from a dysfunctional background, was for many years the most notorious criminal in Scotland. Convicted of murder, he defied every attempt to discipline him. Then one day someone with insight sent him to the special unit at Barlinnie prison. There the staff treated him differently. There he was met and accepted by people like Geoff Shaw, one of the church's finest ministers. The man who once gloried in violence and destruction slowly changed. He began writing poetry and creating sculptures. In his autobiography Jimmy Boyle writes, "I changed the moment I was accepted as a human being."

Caring love quickens the insight. If we are to see rightly, the heart is as important as the eye. Commenting on Jesus' friendships, G. K. Chesterton said, "Jesus never lost his taste for bad company." Instead of poking about in the ashes of people's personalities, he kept looking for the hidden nobilities, the flickering coals, in the hope of fanning them into a warm flame. Not surprisingly, many doubtful characters left his company changed people.

A businessman tells of buying some equipment which did not function properly. For months he tried to get the suppliers to mend it. Finally they sent about the most bedraggled and surly workman imaginable. The businessman would have been justified in being upset at the delay and the workman's attitude. But then he thought, "This fellow was upset and ill-tempered before he got here. There must be many unhappy aspects to his life." So instead of criticising him, he said, "I bet it must be exhausting running round all over the town working on fouled up equipment in this hot weather." On hearing these understanding words, the workman's attitude completely changed. Here was someone who tried to understand his lot. He not only cheerfully carried out the necessary repair, but offered to come back later and check that the machine was still working well.

Everyone hungers for words of appreciation and acceptance.

Non-Scientific Words

Though the best cartoonists think in fun, they often feel in earnest. One of James Thurber's cartoons depicts a man sitting by himself at a party with his head resting on his fist. A guest pointing to the solitary brooder says, "He doesn't know anything except facts." Now there is no denying that facts are important. Scientific facts have been responsible for countless medical and technological advances, and a tremendous growth in human understanding. Scientific inventions have been so numerous and many of them so beneficial, that many have come to believe that science is the final test of all truth, that nothing can be real unless scientifically provable. Science having become the master-light of people's seeing, the lens through which many view everything, it is not surprising that people's awareness that there are other ways of knowing, has been diminished.

Donald Lowrie reminds us that,

> *The most real things we know are all unreal*
> *The firmest, truest all intangible.*
> *Can you weigh mother love as on a scale*
> *Or with a metre measure loyalty?*
> *Can you hold solid justice in your hand*
> *Or with you fingers grasp integrity?*

Though there are no statistics to prove the value of such intangible things as love, loyalty and integrity, many of my most enriching experiences have involved what I would call a 'knowing', not just a feeling. Though I cannot write an equation for the love I feel for my wife and family, or prove their love for me, as I might prove a problem in mathematics, yet the love that binds us is as real to me as food and drink.

Richard Dawkins, who represents the more aggressive strain of atheism, writes "Faith that isn't based on scientific evidence is the principal vice of religion." Is it really? My life, like that of the man in Thurber's cartoon, would be greatly impoverished if that was true, if such crucial dimensions of human existence, represented by such words as faith, hope, love, kindness, trust and beauty were purely figments of the imagination, if only scientific facts were real.

A scientist can tell us the chemical composition of the pigments of a painting. He can date the picture with an accuracy art critics must envy. But when we come to the all-important question, "Is this a work of art?" his laboratory tools are useless. Or think of the crew of a lifeboat risking their lives on a stormy night to rescue stranded sailors. Surely we would not say, "The lifeboat and the waves are real, but there is no way of determining if the crew's courage is real."

To a pathologist who declared that he had examined the human body and could find no trace of a soul, Dr. George Buttrick suggested that when his fellow pathologists examined him when he died, they would find no trace of his consuming passion for medical research. Yet to his friends and medical colleagues few things were more obvious than their colleague's commitment to the advancement of medicine.

We cannot express in a chemical formula Shakespeare's profound insights into human nature, or the forgiving spirit of a Nelson Mandela, or the deep concern of Mother Teresa for the dying in Calcutta, or the feeling we have when someone recognises us and smiles, or the ability to see the point of a joke. Nor can the trustworthiness of a friend be demonstrated in a laboratory. Those content merely to examine a piano or a violin scientifically will never explain the magic of Mozart's music or the haunting beauty of Beethoven's 'Moonlight Sonata'.

At the end of a television programme about the human brain, Professor Robert Winston said, "The human brain is something we can study scientifically. But there is something about it that I cannot account for in scientific terms alone – the phenomenon of consciousness. For this I have to reach for a word outside the sphere of science. I call it ... the soul." Though the scientific mind has greatly enriched our common life, yet by itself the picture it presents of reality is a lopsided one. There is more to life than meets the eye!

Silence

Some years ago the B.B.C. approached the Quakers to see if they might let them record, for broadcasting at a later date, their annual Assembly worship service. But they declined saying, "We fear you will edit out the all-important silences." It is not just the radio that is uncomfortable with silence. Many feel that making time to be quiet is only for the dreamer, the nun and the guru, not for the macho man, or the career woman. Yet how important silence is. Just as the rests in music are as important as the notes, the silent rests being part of the music, so it is in life.

St Paul's Cathedral has been described as an 'isle of silence in a sea of noise.' We need such silent places. The naturalist Henry Thoreau had his 'with-drawing room'. The novelist A. J. Cronin wrote of going into the chapel of Quo Vadis in Rome away from the noise and rush of the city. "There came upon me an extraordinary sense of emptiness and dissatisfaction – an awareness sharp as sudden pain of how fatally I and others like me had become absorbed in worldly affairs. We had forgotten or ignored the Kingdom of the Spirit." Deep within us there are yearnings that are often not heard until we 'study to be quiet'.

Along with the red squirrels, the rain-forests, pandas, tigers and rhinos, silence is also in danger of disappearing from the earth. In 1994 I had the privilege of taking part in the memorial service for the Rt. Hon. John Smith in Westminster Abbey. That day Gerard Manley

Hopkins' poem about the world's wildernesses was read in the service, with its final verse.

What would the world be, once bereft
Of wet and of wildness? Let them be left,
O let them be left, wildness and wet;
Long live the weeds and the wilderness yet.

For John Smith the quiet of Argyll and Iona helped him rediscover his true self and regain perspective. In his busy schedule, these were places of healing.

How important sensitive silences also are in expressing sympathy for those who have suffered greatly. There are occasions which call for that deeper communication of empathy which is possible only through silence. Just as silence is needed to hear a watch tick, so silence can be the medium through which the heartbeats of the heartbroken are better heard. I recall a family where the little girl's favourite doll had been broken by the carelessness of a visiting adult. With the best of intentions the sobbing child's father had said, "Don't worry, I'll buy you a new one." But that did not console her. It was like saying to a mother who has just given birth to a stillborn child, "Oh you are young enough to have another baby", or saying to a man who had lost his dearest friend, "Fortunately you have many other friends." At that moment no newly purchased doll, however marvellous, could make up for the treasured doll upon which so much love had been lavished. The doll lay in pieces, and nothing on earth could make up for the sense of loss. When a few moments later her mother tried to broach the subject, the little girl said, "Don't talk about it now please." She just wanted to be quiet.

The facile words of Job's pious friends and their platitudinous explanations of his immense suffering, his loss of home and cattle, children and health, were to Job's ears a noisy sacrilege. When a colleague said to one of my teachers in America, who had suffered greatly, "You are becoming more and more like Job," he replied, "Perhaps, but I have better friends than Job" – friends who quietly supported him, who knew when to keep silent.

Last Words

Jonathan Swift, the author of *Gulliver's Travels*, was for many years the minister of Dublin Cathedral. Being a sensitive and caring person, he was appalled by the suffering people inflict on one another in the name of patriotism and bad religion. He spoke out often against injustice, bigotry and oppression. In his day it was common for people to write their own epitaphs. I find it significant that he wrote "Jonathan Swift, a champion of human liberty", not "Jonathan Swift, a writer of best sellers."

Thomas Jefferson, the American inventor, architect, philosopher and President, was another who wrote his own epitaph. Once when President Kennedy held a reception in the White House for American Nobel prize winners, he told the assembled gathering that there were probably more brains in the White House that night than ever before. He then paused before adding, "Except perhaps when Thomas Jefferson was here alone." I once visited Monticello, Jefferson's magnificent home in Virginia. Even more fascinating than the display of his amazing inventions, was his tombstone in the garden. His epitaph reads, "Here lies Thomas Jefferson, author of the Declaration of Independence , founder of the University of Virginia and author of the statute of religious freedom for Virginia." No mention is made of the fact that he had been President of the United States. He obviously felt that was not as important as his other achievements.

Some years ago American undertakers introduced 'talking tombstones', tombstones that tell the world what you would like said about you. Naturally you have to record the message before you die! The playback mechanism is powered by solar energy. Though I have grave reservations about talking tombstones, they do pose the question, what would we choose out of our lives as worth remembering?

In a Peanuts cartoon, Linus throws a stick for Snoopy to retrieve. His first dog-instinct is to do what is expected of him, chase the stick. But he finally decides against that. "After I am gone," he says, "I want people to have more to say about me than just 'He was a nice guy. He chased sticks.'" Though most of us would not want as our epitaph, "He was a nice guy. He chased fame and fortune," yet how many sacrifice health, family and principles to attain these very things.

There are two great beginnings in life – the day we are born, and the day we discover why we were born, what is the real purpose of life. The ends for which we live are more important than the means by which we live. It was this understanding of life that Jesus of Nazareth sought to communicate to some Galilean fishermen – that life is for service, not survival, for self-giving, not self-glorification.

Shortly before his assassination, Martin Luther King, the Nobel Peace Prize winner, said, "If any of you are around when I die, I don't want a long funeral. If you get somebody to deliver a eulogy, tell him not to talk too long. Tell him not to mention any of the awards that have been conferred on me – that is not important.

But I would like somebody to say on that day that Martin Luther King did try to feed the hungry, to clothe the naked, to visit those in prison, that he did try to love and serve humanity. Yes and if you want to, say I was a drum major for righteousness, and all the other shallow things will not matter." It is for these things that Martin Luther King is remembered and honoured today. Two thousand years have passed since Jesus of Nazareth walked the hills of Palestine, yet still he is referred to as 'the man for others', 'the friend of publicans and sinners', the 'light of the world'.

The poet Robert Frost wanted engraved on his tombstone the words, "I had a lover's quarrel with the world." Frost nagged and chided the world because he longed to see its rich possibilities realised, its promise fulfilled and its goodness evoked. I warm to St. Augustine's observation concerning the need for both courage and anger – "anger at the way things are and courage to see that they do not remain the way they are."

That was the outlook of Lord Soper, the distinguished Methodist minister. For more than sixty years Donald Soper stood each Sunday afternoon at the gates of Hyde Park answering people's questions about life, politics and religion. During a visit to London in November 1994 my wife and I decided one Sunday to go for a walk in Hyde Park. To my amazement, there at Speaker's Corner was Dr. Donald Soper, aged 92, his mind still rapier sharp. To one heckler who asked him if going the second mile was not in fact the sum and substance of Christianity, Dr. Soper replied. "That is at best a half-truth. But if that is to be the basis of your philosophy, make sure you are heading in the right direction!"

At his memorial service in Westminster Abbey, Tony Benn said of him, "Donald Soper was totally committed to the cause of peace and social justice. He said what he believed and believed what he said. In a world of weathercocks whirling in the wind of fashion, he was a signpost." Though Dr. Soper lived in the first secular age of history, he firmly believed life ought to swing on an ethical hinge.

It was said of a Dr. Hugo Turner when he died that he so wanted to be all things to all people, that 'Turner' was not only the proper, but the inevitable name for him. The corkscrew shaped his course, as it does many today. In order not to stand out, many will do almost anything to fit in. Dr. Soper was critical of what has been called our 'Gallup Poll morality'.

During that exceptionally cruel period in German history, when the Christian faith was in danger of being absorbed into a Christian-Nazi ideology, and the Cross was in danger of being twisted into a swastika, some very courageous members of the German Confessional church met in conference in Barmen. There they produced the famous Barmen Declaration which in essence was a call to Christians to resist the claims of the Third Reich. The authors of the Declaration were upset that the majority of German Protestants were celebrating Hitler as their Führer (leader). They were not only rejecting everything 'Jewish', but introducing into the church's life a crude mixture of pagan and pseudo-Christian elements, including the belief that the Germans were the Master race, created to rule the world. Albert Einstein was deeply moved by the courage of those members of the Confessional Church, who were well aware that their Declaration could well be the last words they would ever write. Einstein wrote, "Only the Confessional Church stood squarely against Hitler's campaign for suppressing truth. I never had any special interest in the Church before, but now I feel a great affection and admiration, because the Church alone has had the courage and persistence to stand for intellectual truth and moral freedom."

Every Duck Praises its own Marsh

Many uncomplimentary things have been said about Scotland and the Scots. The Scottish character has been likened to the Scottish climate – stern and wild. Daniel Defoe, the author of *Robinson Crusoe*, described the Scots as a 'hardened, refractory and terrible people.' Some believe the words 'dour', 'thrawn' and 'crabbit' were in fact coined to describe us.

In Russia, a country which also has St. Andrew as its patron saint, there is a proverb which reads, "Every duck praises its own marsh". That is what I intend to do in this final chapter. I want to respond to such unfair comments about Scotland and my fellow Scots by extolling the glories of a land full of seductive charm. In the customary spirit of Scottish native arrogance I intend to tell you what a fine people we are, and how we are justified in having a 'guid conceit of ourselves'! "I am a Britisher by law," said a Perthshire man, "a Scotsman by birth, and a Highlander by the grace of God." I should add that that same man was sure God's favourite colour was tartan! Another not very modest Scot said, "We are the greatest wee nation God ever put breath into." Another who lived for a period in England, but often returned to Scotland by the overnight train, declared that you could tell when you crossed the border by the more jubilant sound of the train wheels!

Scots at their most defiant have often flung down the challenge, "Here's tae us. Wha's lyke us? Gey few an' they're a' deid!" I suppose, when translated, that really means that the only people we Scots can possibly aspire to emulate are our deceased forebears. Certainly we owe them a tremendous debt. They were obviously people of quality for in many lands a Scottish accent is still an open sesame to a very warm welcome.

Tartan Day

Each April, Americans hold a special Tartan Day. The month of April was chosen for this celebration because April 1320 is the date of the famous Declaration of Arbroath, a Declaration that four hundred years later provided the model for the American Declaration of Independence. What wonderful innovations Scots have given the world – penicillin, beta blockers, tarmacadam, steam engines, the great Clyde-built liners, the telephone and television, to list just a few. Historians marvel at the amazing contribution of Scots to the Age of Enlightenment, the incredible eruption of Scottish genius in the latter part of the 18th century and the early part of the 19th century – a great galaxy of Scottish philosophers, writers, scientists, explorers, engineers, inventors. Churchill said, "Of all the small nations of the earth, perhaps only the ancient Greeks surpass the Scots in their contribution to mankind."

I sometimes get the impression there are two kinds of people – those of Scottish ancestry, and those who would like to have Scottish ancestors! Though Scotland counts only five million people at home, beyond her shores there is a greater Scotland, a much larger group of people who proudly claim Scottish descent. John Buchan, who was born in Perth and educated at Glasgow University, told how it was when he went to live in Oxford that he came to value his Scottish heritage. "As a temporary exile I adopted all the characteristics of a Scot abroad. I cultivated a sentiment for all things Scottish. I became a fervent admirer of Burns." The further Scottish people go from Scotland the more Scottish many of them become. St Andrew's societies and Burns clubs flourish in most corners of the world. The sound of the bagpipes can be heard in many a foreign land. I recall speaking at a St Andrew's day dinner in Winnipeg. That night there were 700 men present, ninety percent of them in full Highland dress.

I personally am proud to belong to the same nation as Robert Burns, James Watt, Alexander Graham Bell, John Logie Baird, Alexander Fleming, Thomas Telford, Charles Rennie Mackintosh, Robert Louis Stevenson, Mary Slessor, Sandy Lyle and Sir Chris Hoy, to mention just a few. The role of Scots who emigrated to America was proportionately far beyond their numbers. Though they formed only seven percent of the colonial population they provided nine of the 56 signatories of the Declaration of Independence. Two of the five members of George Washington's first Cabinet were of Scottish stock. Four Presidents of the United States – Monroe, Hayes, Grant and Wilson were descendants of Scottish immigrants. It was intrepid Scottish explorers like Mungo Park, David Livingstone, and William Balfour Baikie who mapped and opened up large parts of the continent of Africa, Simon Fraser who explored

Western Canada and General Lachlan Macquarie from the little island of Ulva, who opened up parts of Australia. The Macquarie River and County are named after him. I rejoice that it was a Scotsman who founded the Bank of England, another who edited the first edition of the twenty-volume Oxford English Dictionary and yet another who was responsible for the production of the ancient equivalent of Google, the *Encyclopaedia Britannica*. Brilliant minds have been Scotland's best export to the world.

Let me try and shed a little light on the distinction between the words "Scotch", "Scottish" and "Scots". The term Scotch was at one time widely used in Scotland, but for somewhat complex reasons it came to be disliked. Scotch is now used mainly when referring to whisky, tomatoes and other commodities. The term "Scottish" is the equivalent of Irish, Welsh and English. We talk of the Scottish climate, Scottish history, Scottish scenery and the like. We do not talk however of a Scottish man, but of a Scotsman or a Scot. Sometimes the term Scots is used instead of Scottish. For example one invariably talks of Scots Law. It is all very confusing.

The Weather

When Scots meet, more often than not the weather is the first topic of conversation. Whereas other countries have climate, we have weather, weather that changes so often that we always have something to talk about. In one of Burns' songs, beloved the world over, the tenor sings – "I will love thee still, my dear, till a' the seas gang dry." What a protestation of fidelity that is, for there is simply no danger that the seas will dry up as long as Scotland's rain is here to replenish them. Not many are surprised to learn that the band 'Wet, Wet, Wet' comes from Scotland. One very wet summer a Perthshire farmer told a friend he was thinking of changing his postal code from PH2 to H2O. I can sympathise with him and with the Scotsman who paraphrased the well-known Scottish hymn 'O God of Bethel by whose hand thy people still are fed', to read,

O God of Scotland by whose hand
The rain comes tumbling down
Give us we pray just one fine day
Before thy servants drown.

O spread your brolly o'er our heads
To keep our children dry
The weather we have had of late
Brings tears to my glass eye.

The forecast tells of further rain
And drizzle thick as fog
We havenae left the house for days
And neither has the dog.

Despite the rain, I love Scotland. When the sun does shine, Scotland is bonnie beyond words. William Tell's son once asked his father, "Are there any countries where there are no mountains?" When he was told that there were such countries, the lad's sympathies went out to those who lived there. I love the grandeur of our majestic Scottish mountains, the bald sugar-lump of

Suilven, the hefty humpback of Ben Nevis, Perthshire's Schiehallion, and the multi-peaked Ben Loyal. I love them even when swirled about with mist. I also love what Robert Louis Stevenson called 'the essential silence' of our straths and glens, and the clear sparkling rivers flowing through them. One of my pet hates is to see Scotland's natural beauty being defaced by litter. A notice attached to a tree on the Ayrshire Coastal Path near Culzean Castle appealed to me.

"Be ye Man – or Bairn – or Wumman
Be ye gaun – or be ye comin
For Scotland's Pride – no Scotland's shame
Gather your litter – and take it hame."

The Royal Dornoch Golf Course is one of the oldest and most beautiful courses in the world. In 1986 I was Convener of the Club when the British Amateur golf championship was held there. I remember speaking to one of America's leading contenders, Duffy Waldorf. Duffy hailed from Los Angeles. He had arrived early in Dornoch to familiarise himself with links golf. When I asked him how his practising was going, he said – "I have not started practising yet. I am just soaking up the scenery." He quickly fell in love with Sutherland's hills and valleys. He loved Dornoch's sandy beaches laundered each day by wave and wind, and her long summer twilights. Accustomed to the high temperatures and humidity of American summers, Duffy had quickly fallen in love with our much cooler climate and fresh sea breezes. He was full of praise for Scotland.

I love the story (probably apocryphal) about John, a Scottish lad whose grandfather was seriously ill in a

London hospital. Being very fond of his grandfather he decided to take a few days holiday to visit him. Unable to afford the bus or train fare, he cycled. When he arrived at the London hospital it was a very warm sticky day. What a welcome he received from his grandpa, who was sweating profusely. "Oh," said his grandpa, "I would give anything for a breath of good Scottish air." On hearing this, John said, "I think I can grant your wish grandpa." Dashing down the stairs he took off the front wheel of his bicycle. Carrying the wheel up to the ward, he put the valve into his grandpa's mouth, and then released it. Within a minute his grandfather was dead. To the doctors and nurses who came running, the lad explained what had happened, that he had sought to grant his grandpa's request for a breath of good Scottish air. He had no sooner said this than the colour drained from his face. "Oh Doctor," he said, "I forgot I had a puncture at Birmingham."

A Bundle of Contradictions

Scots deny easy classification. We are not all Rob Roys. We don't all wear the kilt. We don't all have red hair. There are as many sides to our character as there are checks in a tartan plaid. We are a bundle of contradictions, or as someone said 'a confusing agglomeration'. After ordering a double cheeseburger with French fries, we Scots then ask for a diet coke. We leave cars worth thousands of pounds out on the driveway, and lock our lawn-mowers and junk in the garage. Despite the fact that Andrew Carnegie gave away more money to good causes than probably any other person, we are known in many corners of the world for our stinginess – or if you wish to be more polite, our thrift. We are known as people who will only cast their bread on the waters if the tide is coming in. One commentator said that the difference between a Scotsman and a canoe is that a canoe occasionally tips.

Scottish stinginess is however a grotesque libel. I am told Scots donate as much per person to charity as any other nation in the world. One of the glories of Scotland is the warmth of its welcome and hospitality. Not for nothing is Scotland known as 'the land of pancakes and scones'. The hospitable Highland greeting "Come awa' ben", has its origin in the old Highland croft houses, commonly called but and bens. The but was the room into which you took the more official guests like the doctor or minister or insurance agent. The ben was the family room into which close and trusted friends were welcomed. I also love the equally incomparable Highland farewells, "Haste ye back" and "Now wouldn't it be a fine thing if you were coming instead of going." I suspect the reason why the Glencoe massacre stirred such a sense of outrage was because it was a betrayal of Scottish hospitality, thirty-eight Macdonalds being slain by soldiers whom they had welcomed into their homes.

The Thistle and Lion Rampant

I question whether the thistle, accompanied as it often is with the motto, "*Nemo me impune lacessit*," which could be paraphrased "I'll jag you if you touch me", is really a valid symbol of the Scottish character. No one would deny that there are a few Scots with a very short fuse. Eric Brown, who in the 1950s was one of Scotland's outstanding professional golfers, was such a person. He was renowned for raging on the golf course at small injustices or bad luck. In the Ryder Cup at Lindrick in 1957 he was drawn on the final day to play the American Tommy Bolt, whose reputation for breaking clubs or throwing them around, had given rise to the nicknames 'Thunder Bolt' and 'Lightning Bolt'. When both players were late in arriving on the first tee, someone suggested that they were probably still on the practice ground, throwing clubs at each other! Though there are some grumpy Scottish Victor Meldrews with firecracker tempers, I really don't think that on average we Scots are more prickly than any other nation.

The lion rampant is probably a more accurate symbol than the thistle. Sir Walter Scott was certain the Scottish character showed to best advantage in adversity. He was probably right. After victory at El Alamein, General Montgomery was heard to say that the perfect blend for a British army was to have one Scot for every two Englishmen! "The Scot is necessary," he said, "to keep the English going forward." A Second World War cartoon depicted a Scottish soldier saying, "You know Willie, if the English surrender, we Scots might have a bit of a fight on our hands." The old ballads portray the Scots as 'bonnie fechters'. Many of our heroes – Braveheart, Robert the Bruce, John Knox and the Covenanters – were prepared to fight rather than accept the overlordship of another nation, or the divine right of corrupt kings, or the exorbitant privileges of a greedy aristocracy. We owe a tremendous debt to John Knox, a man who spearheaded a revolution not with the sword but with tongue and pen. Knox has had a terrible press, being often portrayed as a morose Scottish Orangeman, or dour Scottish ayatollah. For some Knox is the name given to all that they dislike in religion. He is thought of as shorthand for grim repressive Calvinism. But in fact Knox was a far more convivial character than the dark stereotypes, paintings and sculptures of him. As far as dress was concerned he was one of the great dandies of his day. He was a man of wide sympathies, and much humour. Harry Reid in his book about the Reformation says of Knox: "He was emphatically not the killjoy of popular caricature". Nor was he the destroyer of Scottish culture. I warm to the suggestion of one of his biographers that when Knox spoke of the monstrous regiment of women he was at that time living with his mother-in-law!

Knox's great dream was that there should be a school in every parish in Scotland where children would have free education. He wanted funds established so that promising youngsters, the 'lads o' pairts', could go to university. Our Scottish education system owes a tremendous debt to John Knox. Andrew Herman in his modern classic *How the Scots Invented the Modern World*, calls the Scots the schoolmasters of Europe. I find it significant that for a long time Scotland had four universities compared to England's two, Oxford and Cambridge.

Fiddle Music

At a St Andrew's day dinner in Indonesia at which I had been invited to propose the toast to Scotland, I glimpsed tears running down several faces of exiled Scots as they listened to the pipers, and to fiddlers playing well-known Scottish songs. Memories of their homeland and kinsfolk were stirred. Most Scottish people have a softer nature than the 'Scots wha hae' image. Their emotions often lie close to the surface.

In the 17th century many of the Kirk's ministers thundered against those who played the fiddle. Harps were acceptable, being associated with heaven, but fiddles, because of their link with dancing, were unacceptable. This situation continued until the beginning of the 18th century when there was enormous enthusiasm for dance music in many European countries. The Scottish upper classes were envious of the freedom their English counterparts enjoyed of dancing to fiddle music. Dance classes were initiated in Edinburgh in the early 18th century. The Kirk lost the battle. One of most influential and earliest exponents of Scottish fiddle music was Niel Gow, a native of Inver in Perthshire.

I love Richard Stillgoe's radio tribute to fiddle music, 'Violin Farm':

A sycamore tree cannot mimic the lark –
A sycamore tree's unaccompanied bark
Is silent until the tree's finally felled,
Seasoned and shaped and then lovingly held
Beneath a Korean or Hungarian chin.
For sycamore's what makes a great violin.

A sheep cannot sing – the song of a sheep
Would shatter a goblet or rouse you from sleep.
But the guts of the sheep, when the sheep's passed away,
Can be twisted and tightened and tuned to an 'A'.
So what started off filling up a sheep's middle
Ends up as strings on the sycamore fiddle.

A horse cannot play you a musical scale
But if you sneak up and you shorten his tail
The hairs, when attached to a suitable rod,
Can play the sheep's guts like the song of a God.
The rest of the horse, if it's under the weather,
Is boiled up to glue the whole thing together.

So if you should pass by a meadow or lea
Where a sheep grazes next to a sycamore tree,
And yonder a horse canters, tail in the air –
You'll know the true meaning beneath what lies there.
You can say to the kids, with a wave of your arm,
"What you see over there is a violin farm".

Scott and Burns

I never cease to marvel at the marked contrast in backgrounds between the two Scotsmen who put Scotland on the literary map – Scotland's most famous storyteller Sir Walter Scott, who burned himself out trying to repay debts incurred by his publisher, and Scotland's finest poet Robert Burns, who died at an even earlier age. Both had a profound love of Scotland.

Scott's historical fiction highlighted the richness and grandeur of Scotland's heritage. Scott wrote,

Breathes there the man, with soul so dead,
Who never to himself hath said,
This is my own, my native land!

By means of stories about the Highland clans and his description of the hills, moors and glens in which they lived and roamed, the laird of Abbotsford illuminated everything Scottish with the flame of romance and pageantry. His novels so enhanced the reputation of Scotland abroad that some referred to Scotland as the land of Scott. Walter Scott is generally regarded as being largely responsible for what has been called 'the torrent of tartanry'. He succeeded in bringing King George IV north of the border to hold court wearing the kilt, a garment which his grandfather had banned after the Jacobite rebellion. Scott said of the kilt, "It is an ancient dress, a martial dress, a becoming dress." Walter Scott was also responsible for later bringing Queen Victoria to Deeside, and the artist Landseer to paint the great 'monarchs' of the Highland glens. After his death in 1832 Scott was commemorated in Princes Street by a colossal monument that would not have looked out of place on the launch pad of an American space centre.

For Robert Burns there was no luxury estate house. He was the son of a toil-worn crofter. Burns suffered at the hands of his father whose nature had been soured by adversity.

It was memories of how his father had suffered at the hands of a cruel local factor, that caused him to write in his poem "The Twa Dogs",

Poor tenant bodies, scant o' cash
How they maun thole a factor's snash;
He'll stamp an' threaten, curse an' swear
He'll apprehend them, poind (impound) *their gear*

I smiled on hearing how in an essay about Burns, a little girl wrote that he was born, not in Alloway, but in an alley way. Though his birthplace was not as impoverished as that , it was certainly in a lowly 'but and ben' that he spent his early years. Yet today Burns, more than any other Scot, is recognised not only as Scotland's greatest son, but the voice of the Scottish people. There is a perennial relevance about what he said about the brotherhood of man, the primacy of the home and the hypocrisy of the Holy Willies of this world. He would have loved the remark of the little Scottish boy who was told one day that his great aunt Gladys had died. As well as having no great love for children and seldom smiling, her religion was one of doom and gloom. When his mother informed him that Aunt Gladys had died and had gone to be with God in heaven, the wee lad responded with a sincere look of sympathy, "Poor God."

The Saltire

The Saltire or St. Andrew's Cross has become yet another national symbol. It serves as a reminder of how closely the history of kirk and nation in Scotland has been intertwined. To understand any people it is helpful to understand their religion, what they regard as of ultimate value. Even though that religion may not be practised regularly by the majority, it does affect for better or worse the national outlook. I find it significant that the tie of the Royal and Ancient Golf Club of St. Andrews – the Vatican of Golf – depicts St. Andrew bearing the X-shaped cross on which he was crucified. I cannot help wondering if it is because many golfers suffer so many agonies and disappointments on the golf course that golf's governing body decided to choose as their emblem the figure of a tortured saint. How mistaken wives often are in thinking that every time their husbands are on the golf course they are having enormous fun. For many it is often more pain than fun.

The Haggis and Sport

The haggis with its 'honest sonsie face' has become almost another Scottish icon. No one is quite sure how Scottish patriotism became linked with the lowly haggis, made from the liver, lungs and other parts of a sheep and cow not mentionable in polite company. In a film about Rob Roy, the hero at one point is depicted apparently crawling into the carcass of a cow that has just died. He does this not to hide from his enemies, but to look for some tasty parts to put into a haggis. In her cook-book *The Scots Kitchen*, Dr. Marian McNeill says she cherishes the haggis because it shows how a wise nation can make so much out of left-overs. Alistair Borthwick tells in one of his books that the first time haggis was imported into Canada, it was refused entry as a foodstuff. It was finally only allowed to clear customs under the classification of Fertiliser! I remember also someone saying with tongue in cheek that the haggis demonstrates that to be a true Scot you have to have a lot of guts. With the approach of Burns night a Highland butcher put a notice in his window. "Try our Haggis. You will never get better!" With all the food scares, he could have worded it better.

Sport may be an unsatisfactory means of national expression, but it is another visible and potent measure of a country's identity. It may be illogical to judge a nation's worth by the way its football or rugby team performs, but sport certainly has a powerful effect on morale. When a national team is winning, production goes up, absenteeism drops and at least, for a little, people stop complaining about the weather. Though in Hugh McIlvanney's words Scottish teams "often snatch defeat from the jaws of victory", the loyalty of her supporters scarcely ever wavers. The story goes that when one loyal member of the Tartan Army was job-hunting, in reply to the interviewer's question, "What's your ultimate goal?" he replied, "Archie Gemmell's goal against Holland in the World Cup." His answer was probably the reason he did not get the job.

Scottish Humour

There is one other aspect of the Scottish character which it would be remiss not to mention, and that is the Scottish sense of humour. How refreshingly witty and funny Scottish people can be. What outstanding observational comedians Scotland has produced, comedians like Billy Connolly and Chic Murray. Both had an eye for the sense of the ridiculous and the recurring comedy of everyday things. At the beginning of a skit about church ministers Billy Connolly said, "Faith is like an ash-tray – It is fu' of wee douts" ('douts' being cigarette ends, as well as sounding like 'doubts'). In a programme about Scottish history, he said of Bonnie Prince Charlie, "He is the only man I know who was named after three sheep-dogs." John Webster, a minister friend who lives in the Island of Arran, tells of returning once from the mainland with a family whose mother had died. They were bringing her ashes back for burial in Arran. One of the daughters had noticed Billy Connolly getting on to the boat at Ardrossan. "Oh, Mr. Webster," she said, "My mother just loved Billy Connolly's programmes. Would you be willing to go and ask him if he would come and meet my mother?" Her mother was now a box of ashes! My friend who is a delightful maverick did what I would not have done. He went and explained the situation to Billy Connolly. To his surprise Billy agreed to come back with him. Having shaken hands and sympathised with the daughters in their loss, he then took the box of ashes in his hands and started speaking to the box. "I am awfully glad to meet you. This will be a free voyage for you today. You won't have had to buy a ticket ..." On he went for a full minute talking to her ashes. It was a masterly piece of monologue.

Chic Murray told how one night, having rung the bell of a small Bed and Breakfast on the Ayrshire Coast, a lady appeared at the upstairs window. "What do you want?" she asked. When Chic replied, "I would like to stay here," she replied, "Well stay there," and banged the window shut.

Rab C. Nesbitt is not my favourite Scottish T.V. character. But on one of the few occasions I watched the programme, I had to smile when Rab told his friend how the previous night his wife had clubbed him several times over the head for once again coming home drunk. Then Rab added, "It is wee surprises like that which keeps our marriage alive."

An American who was driving through the Highlands stopped to ask a farmer how far it was to Castle Urquhart. "Well," said the farmer, "the way you are going it is about 25,000 miles. But if you turn around it is only about two."

Another American who was searching for his family roots on Tiree asked a local about the burial customs on the island. He asked if it was true that the family took the coffin around the homes of friends on the morning of the funeral. Trying to conceal a mischievous twinkle in his eye, the old crofter said, "Yes indeed. We stop at the homes of close friends to let them pay their respects to the deceased. In each home a dram is poured." The crofter then went on to explain how the rooms in some of the Tiree croft houses are so small that they often had to stand the coffin on its end. On what could be sometimes a rather lengthy journey to the grave, far too many drams were consumed by the mourners. "That," he said, "explains why so many grandfather clocks have been buried on Tiree."

Most Scottish humour is genial, but occasionally there is a barb in it. One night at a congregational dinner dance in the village hall, the newly inducted young minister and his wife were seen gliding gracefully over the dance floor. After watching their intricate footwork, one of the older members, who felt the minister's sermons lacked substance, was overheard to say to a friend, "The trouble with our minister is that he is educated at the wrong end."

Occasionally, however, the witty barb can be too caustic. It becomes an expression of contempt. During the debate on the famous Salmonella egg controversy, so closely associated with Edwina Currie, or Eggwina Currie as she is now often known, the late Sir Nicholas Fairbairn, the former Conservative M.P. for Perth, came to the defence of the poor egg. "The honourable member," he said, "should remember that she was once an egg. Can I add that the fertilisation of that egg was not an event that enriched the human race."

Love for one's native land is as natural and normal as love of home and family. What praise Shakespeare heaped on the land of his birth – 'this sceptred isle, this other Eden, demi-paradise, this dear, dear land.' The inhabitants of Quito, high up in the Andes have a lovely saying, "After Quito heaven, and in heaven an opening

to look down on Quito." Lovers of Scotland might be tempted to say something similar. Robert Burns expressed his love for his homeland in these moving words, "O Scotia! my dear, my native soil! / For whom my warmest wish to heaven is sent!" Yet, how internationalist Burns also was in his thinking. He gave us a vision of a world where "Man to Man, the world o'er, / Shall brothers be for a' that!"

An army general, who had been driven in a jeep over a very rough battle-field, complimented the driver on his careful driving. Back came the reply, "Well sir, I look at it this way, I am in the jeep too." Though we are justified in having a deep love for our homeland, and cherishing our national heritage, we must never forget that we are inseparably linked to other nations, that we are all in it together. We need each other. We share a common humanity.

Also by James A. Simpson from Steve Savage Publishers

Holy Wit   ISBN 9781904246022 RRP £4.99
'A really happy lttle book'
Northern Times

More Holy Wit   ISBN 9781904246404 RRP £5.95
'A goldmine for after-dinner speakers ... a howling success'
Life and Work

Laughter Lines   ISBN 9781904246282 RRP £4.95
'Crammed with jokes, aphorisms and humorous anecdotes'
The Scotsman

Life, Love and Laughter   ISBN 9781904246046 RRP £5.99
'Full of cracking anecdotes'
Sunday Post

A Funny Way of Being Serious   ISBN 9781904246176 RRP £5.99
'Vintage Simpson – humour, insight, spiritual insight and sacred comment'
Presbyterian Herald

At Our Age   ISBN 9781904246343 RRP £5.95
A glorious collection of pieces related to getting older ... excellent as a gift at any time and not just for the elderly'
The GoodBookstall

Available from bookshops or directly from the publisher.

For information on mail order terms, see our website (www.savagepublishers.com) or write to: Mail Order Dept., Steve Savage Publishers Ltd., The Old Truman Brewery, 91 Brick Lane, LONDON, E1 6QL.